The Pine Island Paradox

KATHLEEN DEAN MOORE

milkweed
editions

Published 2004 by Milkweed Editions
Printed in the United States of America
Jacket and interior design by Christian Fünfhausen
Author photo courtesy of Ball Studio
The text of this book is set in Caslon.
09 5 4 3 2
First Edition

Milkweed Editions, a nonprofit publisher, gratefully acknowledges support from Emilie and Henry Buchwald; Bush Foundation; Cargill Incorporated; DeL Corazón Family Fund; Dougherty Family Foundation; Ecolab Foundation; Joe B. Foster Family Foundation; General Mills Foundation; Jerome Foundation; Kathleen Jones; Constance B. Kunin; D. K. Light; Chris and Ann Malecek; McKnight Foundation; a grant provided by the Minnesota State Arts Board, through an appropriation by the Minnesota State Legislature, a grant from the Wells Fargo Foundation Minnesota, and a grant from the National Endowment for the Arts; Sheila C. Morgan; Laura Jane Musser Fund; National Endowment for the Arts; Navarre Corporation; Kate and Stuart Nielsen; Outagamie Charitable Foundation; Qwest Foundation; Debbie Reynolds; St. Paul Companies, Inc., Foundation; Ellen and Sheldon Sturgis; Surdna Foundation; Target, Marshall Field's, and Mervyn's with support from the Target Foundation; Gertrude Sexton Thompson Charitable Trust; James R. Thorpe Foundation; Toro Foundation; Weyerhaeuser Family Foundation; and Xcel Energy Foundation.

Library of Congress Cataloging-in-Publication Data

Moore, Kathleen Dean.
    The Pine Island paradox / Kathleen Dean Moore.-- 1st ed.
        p. cm.
    ISBN 1-57131-276-5 (hardcover : alk. paper)
    1. Human ecology. 2. Island ecology. 3. Nature. 4. Environmental ethics. 5. Conservation of natural resources. 6. Environmental protection. I. Title.
    GF47.M57 2004
    304.2--dc22

                                                    2003024028

This book is printed on acid-free paper.

The Pine Island Paradox

●

To Frank

The Pine Island Paradox

A COASTAL ISLAND   *sacred / mundane*

All or parts of the following essays have been previously published in slightly different forms or under different titles: "What It Means to Love a Place" in the *Shack*, "Toward an Environmental Ethic of Care" in *Inner Voice*, "The World Depends on This" in the *Oregonian*, "Fire and Water" in *Open Spaces*, "Blowing the Dam" in *Audubon*, "The Inheritance of Acquired Characteristics" in *River*, "The Road to Cape Perpetua" in *Wild Earth*, "This Will Not Come Again" in *Call of the River*, "Finis / Genesis" in *Interdisciplinary Studies in Literature and the Environment*, "Another World Could Start Right Here" in *Hope Magazine*.

The Pine Island Paradox

PROLOGUE

SAY YOU HAVE THE JOB of taking the measure of an island. Say you are a mapmaker. You will need boots and a small boat and a measuring tape. Will you stretch the tape tight around a headland, or will you trace every crevice and acorn barnacle? Will you start when the sea tucks up tight and floods the eelgrass, or when the island spreads out steaming on an ebbing tide? Your task will be harder still if you choose a rainy day or a day of bright wind when waves smack on rock. How will you map the seepage of nitrogen from the alders into the ocean, and the way the haircap moss breathes oxygen that catches in the waves?

On Pine Island, the Alaskan wilderness island where my family camps, I push aside the rubber stems of bull kelp, searching at the edge of water for the place where the land ends and the sea begins. I can stand in the dark heart of the hemlock forest, feet planted firmly on duff, and say, "This is Pine Island," or slosh knee-deep into the bay and say, "This is the Pacific Ocean." But the distinction doesn't hold up at the edges. The more closely I search, the more elusive the edge becomes. Diving cormorants roost in the crown of the red cedar by the bay, but barnacles grow on the roots that rake the water. Are these land or sea, and at what particular time of day or night? How should I classify my wading children, all water and laughter? And what do I make of the places between the high and low tides, these half-island, half-sea slopes of anemones and sea slugs—the gasping, wincing things?

Again and again, I face an island's paradox: Not even an island is an island. Storm-washed and rain-sodden, so hard to get to, so hard to escape, Pine Island is the very symbol of isolation and exile. But any geographer will tell you that an island is in fact only a high point in the continuous skin of the planet, the small part we can see of the hidden substance that connects everything on earth. It's a sign—a beautiful, rock-solid, bird-spattered sign—of the wholeness of being, the intricate interdependencies that link people and places.

WE WHO LIVE in a world mapped by Western philosophy live in a world of islands. While people of wisdom in virtually all other cultures studied the continuities that link human and nature, near and far, the sacred and the mundane into one Whole, Western philosophers were busy making distinctions.

The separations may date from the very beginnings of Western philosophy, on the marble steps of ancient

Greece. Not many of us read Democritus and Leucippus anymore, but not many of us doubt what they taught: that all of reality can be reduced to hard little particles, mechanical substance that humans can measure, understand, manipulate, and ultimately control. But are humans mechanical substance only? To solve that problem, Protagoras dismembered human beings, separating the mind, which is not material, from the body, which is. And because only humans are presumed to have minds, Protagoras severed humans from the rest of nature in the same clean stroke.

The divisions widened during the European Enlightenment. René Descartes separated mind from body, human from animal, user from used. Francis Bacon separated culture from nature and transformed knowledge into power over the natural world. Capitalist economics transformed the natural world into a commodity. Immanuel Kant insisted that moral duties are imposed by abstract principle, divorced from natural inclination or love. Thomas Hobbes and John Locke argued that humans are essentially individual, related to others through competition for individual rights. Even nature writers—count Henry David Thoreau first among them—taught that only when people leave society and walk alone in the wildness will they find strength and truth.

A philosophy professor myself, I read these books in my own department—separated from biology, which is across the street, and history, two blocks east and up three flights of stairs.

And yet, my own experience is of connection. My life

is blessed by islands: tide-washed Pine Island, no bigger than a K-Mart parking lot. A nameless yellow-poppy gravel bar in the Willamette River that flows past my town. Rocky bird sanctuaries off the Oregon coast. Here especially, on these islands, I feel most completely part of the natural world and most closely connected to my family, sitting on stones with our feet in the water, watching gulls swirl over herring that turn and flash in the sun.

I listen to the slosh of the sea and the cry of a fish crow in cedars just starting to rustle in afternoon winds. From far away come the voices of my daughter and son, the creak of an oar, the bump of a boat—all the quiet music of an island in the tide. What is the place of human beings in the harmony of the whole, and what does that tell us about how we ought to act in the world?

IN THIS BOOK, I want to take the measure of three *insulae*, three separations drawn onto the worldviews of the Western world. The first is the claim that human beings are separate from, and superior to, nature. If we understand instead that humans are seamlessly connected, are kin, to the natural world, then we might act in more caring ways toward the earth and all its inhabitants. Thus, part one of the book, "An Island in the Tides, human/nature."

The second "island" is the separation between what is near in time and space from what is far away, the illusion that our individual well-being can be disconnected from the well-being of the biological and social systems that sustain us—the air we breathe, the water we drink, the land we harvest, and the local and global communities we live in. If we understand instead that our lives are seamlessly connected to the biocultural whole, then we might find our own integrity, acknowledging that the special care we take of our own interests and homes, we owe also to the future and to the larger world. Thus part two of the book, "An Island in the River, near/far."

The third is the separation of the mundane from the sacred, the idea that we live in a material world that has only instrumental value, apart from the sacred, the intrinsically valuable, which exists on a different plane, if it exists at all. If we believe instead that the mundane is sacred, then rather than devalue what we have and yearn for a better place, we might be more attentive to what is wonderful on this earth, living with joy and gratitude. This is the theme of part three of the book, "A Coastal Island, sacred/mundane."

GEOGRAPHERS MAKE ELABORATE maps of the earth, using aerial photographs and bits of data from satellites. These maps are artifacts of great beauty, the vivid lines and pixels and sweeps of color. Then geographers go to the places they have mapped, to follow the rivers and walk transects across the land. Their job is to ground-truth the maps, to link the map's abstract patterns to the actuality of the ground—the feel of it, the forests and towns, the estuaries and the bright edge of water.

I want to do the ground-truthing work of environmental ethics, to pull on rubber boots and follow the ebb tide into the tidal flats—listening, asking questions, poking around, exploring the place where clams squirt fountains and children laugh out loud, getting a sense of the whole of the land, trying in some small way to understand who I am in this time and place, and what I ought to do.

AN ISLAND IN THE TIDES

human / nature

Geography

The Pacific Coast of Canada and southeast Alaska is a mountain range carved by glaciers into knife ridges and shadowed valleys. Nine million years ago, snow built up on the mountains, compressed into ice, and slowly slid downhill, scraping against bedrock, gouging steep canyons. In some places, the river of ice split, carving a high prominence between the valleys. Then the glaciers melted, leaving tumbled rock and a landscape of dramatic cliff faces, rock slides, pointed peaks, ridges, and hanging valleys with waterfalls dropping to the riverbed.

Eventually, the whole continental shelf subsided, sinking the coastal mountains and valleys below sea level. As salt water flooded the valleys, only the highest points of land remained dry. This is the landscape of the fjord country, where fingers of the Pacific Ocean reach deep into the valleys between inland mountains. Small islands cluster beside steep ridges that climb to snow-capped peaks or fall away in abrupt cliffs. Pine Island is the westernmost in this cluster of islands.

Standing on Pine Island, it's not hard to imagine

yourself standing on the tip of a mountain, the valleys below filled, not with hemlocks and bears, but snow crabs and silt, and sea stars clinging to the kelp-draped cliffs.

THE AUGMENTED FOURTH

RAIN DRUMMED ON THE HATCHES and splashed off the decks, but still we could make out the sound of a wolf howling from the cliffs over the cove where we dropped anchor. There was only one wolf, although we listened carefully to be sure. The howl started low, leapt up, slid along the water, and sank away. Nothing answered the wolf's call. Frank and I listened, as the wolf must have listened, the question probing the clouds and damping out in the forest, the draperies of lichens and drooping hemlock boughs.

But the only response was rain pounding, then rivering down my sleeves and soaking my gloves. I tucked my hands into my sleeves, ducked my head, and hunched my shoulders to direct the water down my raincoat instead, to the deck of the boat and off the stern to the sea. The wolf howled again. I knelt to raise the anchor so we could drift closer to the cliff.

I knew the song the wolf sang. The first two tones made an augmented fourth, a dissonant interval, like the first two notes of "Maria" in *West Side Story*. It's an interval of yearning, of hope—the sound of human longing.

When my colleague, a concert pianist, explained the augmented fourth, she brought both hands together in front of her body, palms skyward, fingers spread, and lifted the air. For her, words are not enough to describe this interval. This is a sound that floods the soul, she said, and she strained forward from the waist. The augmented fourth is a heartbreaking interval, dissonance that comes so close to consonance, pulls itself so close, but never reaches the perfect fifth that is almost within its grasp.

She leaned over the keyboard and played two notes: C, F-sharp. Then she flooded the room with music made of the unfinished intervals, harmonies that lead toward resolution but never reach a place of peace. Tony, reaching for Maria. A Greek chorus pleading with the gods to have mercy on Orestes' soul, this man who has murdered his mother. Tristan, yearning for the white sail that will bring his beloved Isolde on a following wind. And Robert Schumann, poor lovesick Schumann, yearning for Clara. *Yearning:* this ancient word, diving straight through history from the beginnings of language itself, a word as old as *home* or *earth*. No one in Christian medieval Europe sang the augmented fourth, my colleague said. It was the *diabolus in musica*, the devil's chord—so powerful it could grab a parishioner, drag him to his knees and pull him, scraping on the paving stones, straight to hell. And there I was in that tide-dragged island wilderness, also on my knees, trying to understand the pull of these same two notes.

I sat on my heels and strained to hear the wolf again, but the rain defeated me. There must have been three rainstorms stacked above us: A grayness in the air that wetted every surface, even under the canopy, soaking our hair but barely dimpling the water. An overloaded cloud dropping rain like sand from a shovel. And one unbearably heavy cloud that held the rain until it broke loose in huge drops that raised welts on the sea.

Listening intently, we pulled in our rockfish jigs and let the boat drift among small islands, until finally the dusk turned into dark. Then Frank started up the engine and slowly steered us back to Pine Island where we had made camp.

THERE IS NO DARKER NIGHT than a night of rain on an island. Frank played his flashlight beam over the inlet to make sure the boat was still resting at anchor. I sat on an overturned bucket under a tarp stretched between hemlocks. Under my boots, the ground was springy, a thick layer of moss on a century of hemlock needles. Rain poured onto the tarp, pooling in a corner that sagged until the edge of the tarp let loose, dashing the water to the ground. The tarp rebounded, spattering drops that sizzled against the lantern and wet my cheeks. I pulled my bucket closer to the center of the tarp. Even under its shelter, it was hard to stay out of the rain. Water bounced off the stems of highbush blueberries and salal, dripped from every stray end of rope, runnelled the length of hemlock roots. I sat hunched, forearms resting on knees, and drank whiskey, closely rationed.

Somewhere people were laughing in brightly lit places that smelled of books and coffee. Families were sitting down to dinner, somewhere, and fishermen were making fast their boats in harbors, calling out to friends as they hoisted their gear bags to their shoulders and turned toward home. But there were no other people here, and not another point of light for fifty miles in all directions. Tonight, just our little family, and in my flashlight beam, a narrow strip of island rapidly sinking into a flooding tide.

A loud mournful wail. I was on my feet, reaching for binoculars, but of course there was nothing to see in that darkness. It sounded again—a musical arch of three tones. I ducked past the tarp and groped to the edge of the island, and there was the call again. I recognized the wail of a common loon. Waking at night, the loon might have found itself suddenly alone, or in the storm lost sight of its mate. It called again with frantic urgency; first, two sustained tones, the second higher and longer—two wavering tones on that rainy night after so many days of rain. Then it added another interval, even higher and longer. That was the wild, heartbreaking sound of the augmented fourth.

I yanked off my hood and turned my face toward the call. The loon flew toward me, then veered suddenly, and the cry slowly faded away. I strained forward, trying so hard to hear an answering call. What I heard was water on water and the slosh of tide on rock.

I should have felt a loneliness close to despair, there, in the night, in the rain, a thousand miles from home. What I felt instead was uncommon joy. What was there to long for, where all I wanted was what I suddenly had?— to be fully part of the night, joined by a song, by a simple shared song, to the loon, to the wolf, to the keening of all humankind, all of us together in this one infinite night, all of us floating in the same darkness, each of us, as we howl our loneliness, finding that we are not alone after all.

STALKING SEALS

WE WOKE UP TO the cover of thick white fog, exactly
what I needed. Ever since we landed on the island, we'd
been watching harbor seals. Or maybe it's more accurate
to say they had been spying on us. They hung around at
the edge of our range of focus and looked toward our
tents. Through binoculars, we could see their little round
heads and big baby's eyes emerging from the water. But
even when we couldn't see them, at night or when clouds
sank into the cedars, we could hear them. A harbor seal
in the distance growls like a bear, especially when your
ears are tuned to bear and the bears are big and plentiful.
A seal growls like a stomach too, when you have limited
your diet to pasta on the dubious principle that whatever food is unattractive to you will also be unattractive
to bears. We sat on rocks at the prow of the island, trying
to locate the sounds, scanning the sea with binoculars,
then glancing over our shoulders for any movement in
the bushes. We laughed at ourselves for not knowing the
difference between a harbor seal and a brown bear and
our own hunger. But when we trained binoculars on the

seals, they seemed to feel the heat of the gaze, and when we stared, they sank out of sight.

Day after day we watched them from a distance. They hung out on a rock pile just two islands down the channel. At high tide, the rocks disappeared and the seals bobbed in the water, blowing bubbles and snorting. But at low tide, especially at night, the seals heaped on the rocks in gray, rigid curves—sighing and grumbling and growling, or when something disturbed them, crying like seagulls in a dump.

I tried repeatedly to paddle a kayak close to them on their rocks, but each time they knew I was coming. Some sentinel always gave the alarm, and they humped in a panic to the edge of the rock, heaved themselves overboard, and sank out of sight. I came in friendship, but how do you convey intention to a harbor seal? I thought later that I should have left offerings on the island—silvery fish heads, glistening blue necklaces of entrails and bracelets of feathery gills. But I never thought of it then.

After days of trying, getting close to the seals became an obsession. My feelings were hurt when they didn't trust my efforts to make friends. Maybe they had reasons to distrust human beings, but I wanted only to get close—to smell their breath and listen to their stomachs growl and make trails with my fingers in the fish-oil slick around the island, or watch their mouths work while they dreamed. In my imagination, I could slide my body over the rocky barnacles, dragging suddenly useless legs, and lay my head on a sleeping seal's soft flank. But when I approached over rocks, they belched in my general direction and fled.

It is a heartache, honestly, to be so shunned. I have never understood why a creator god would go to so much trouble to separate one thing from another—the light from the darkness, waters that were under the firmament from waters that were above, the seas from the dry land, and worst of all, humankind from the fishes of the sea and the birds of the air and every creeping thing. Myself, I like the magical, mixed, god-saturated things that somehow escaped the Great Separations—dusk and fog, marshland and mudflats, dawn, and chickadees that feed from my hand.

I think the reason we come to Pine Island each summer—Frank and I and our grown kids, if they can find the time—is to leave behind the routines and pride and presuppositions that separate us from the natural world. We sink into the creeping greenness of this place, the pull of tides and splash of sun, the sighing seals and sucking starfish, living for a while among the oblivious abundance of other lives. I admit, it's not always an easy place to be. Wildness means driving rain and mosquitoes, slippery rocks and barnacles that can tear the skin off boats. The fact is, it's often lonely. But by the end of the school year, I'm hungry for this. I pack gear and repair boats with the same urgency I feel when I'm going to visit my children. But I'm away from wildness so long that I always seem to come as an intruder to this place—if kin to the brown bears, then a loud-mouthed, piano-legged aunt who arrives unbidden with all her baggage. Like that aunt, I was determined to get close to those harbor seals.

Since the direct assault clearly wasn't going to succeed, I tried to be creative. I set my baseball cap on backwards, hoping the seals would think I was paddling away. They didn't. I sat in my kayak, pointed the bow away from the island and paddled backward toward them. Of course, the seals sank away from me.

But that morning, all the bay was concealed by a cover of whiteness. No chance the seals would see me; I couldn't see even the bow of my kayak, four feet away. There was no wind to carry the terrifying metallic smell of a human being. If I was as quiet as water, just a rustle, they wouldn't hear me come. I would float with the outgoing tide—a piece of kelp, a Styrofoam worm carton—until I nudged against the island piled with sleeping seals.

Softly into the water. Softly through the fog on the breath of the tides. I pivoted quietly in the currents, my paddle stowed. Strands of kelp floated along beside me. The sun lifted over the islands, a lens of brightness in bright air. I couldn't be sure I was moving; the whole bay gradually tilted toward the sea, and I was sliding with the glass-smooth water on the slipping tide. For the longest time, there was no sound. Then I heard water lisping against the island. A smell like decaying fish spread through the fog. After a few minutes, I could see an oily slick on the water. I was getting close. I heard a seal's wet, fluttering sneeze.

Then straight out of the water—two huge round heads with bulging, white-rimmed eyes. The seals came at me so quickly that I snatched up my paddle, back-paddled as fast as I could, then dug in a hard stroke and turned to race away. I could hear them pushing through the water behind me. Paddling, paddling, remembering how big a harbor seal is, how easily it can overturn a kayak, how violently it slaps apart a salmon, I pulled hard for a small island that would hide me.

Finally, I turned the headland and lay in among rocks in shallow water. My shoulders ached and I struggled to catch my breath. The fog had lifted into low clouds. The bay shone silver as a nickel, and as flat, except for my own wake following me around the corner. The world was utterly silent. Gradually, my breathing returned to normal and the tide began to slacken, settling into glossy quiet, the kelp arrayed now in random directions, long fronds floating. I leaned back against the deck.

That's when I heard heavy breathing behind me. I spun the kayak around, but there was nothing there, and then the breathing was behind me again. Again, I spun the kayak around. Nothing. I shot across open water, skidded into the bay, and ran the kayak onto the gravel beach at camp.

❋

I DID GET CLOSE to the seals that summer, but it was entirely by accident, and I didn't so much get close to them as they came close to me. I was floating on a slack tide around the back of the island because I wanted to be alone, and I was crying. No point in making too much of this. If you've spent weeks in steady rain under clouds that turn the hemlocks black, or if the rain finally stops and you're weepy from the gift of a weak and watery sun, or for no reason: Sometimes when you're far away from home, you cry, that's all. So that's what I was doing. Just sitting motionless in my kayak, eyes squeezed shut, snuffling, letting the soggy intertidal salt-weed moisture seep into my own misery. After a while, I was done. When I looked up, I found I was closely surrounded by seals. Big seals, little seals, all watched without comment, their black nostrils beading water, their round heads so close they could have pressed nose-prints in the dew on my hull.

Not approaching, not avoiding, the seals rose and fell gently on the swell, as I rose and fell, the soft sounds of our breathing a language we shared. What would make us human beings think we're something radically different from the other inhabitants of the natural world? Or if different, what grand leap of logic or arrogance would make us think we're superior? And even if we were superior, what right would that grant to dominate the world, to have our way with it? That day, it felt like a true, good thing, to float with the seals on the incoming tide, staring frankly at one another with our watery, red-rimmed eyes.

WHAT IT MEANS TO LOVE
A PLACE

ETHEL ISN'T OUR big boat's real name. It's a nickname, an acronym that stands for equipment hassles from hell. Frank objects strenuously. It's bad luck to rename a boat, he always says, and besides, ETHEL isn't a proper acronym; you can't just take whatever letters you want out of whatever words seem appropriate and put them together to serve your own purposes. Our daughter Erin says "ETHEL" creates terrible karma. Showing anything but absolute respect for a boat sends chills down her back, and naming the misfortune you fear, she says, will bring it down on your head. Maybe she's right: If we want to rename the boat, we should be careful and call it something lucky, like Grace. Or Safely Home.

But ETHEL is the name that stuck, good luck or bad, like any nickname. And ETHEL has earned its name a hundred times over. During the winter, squirrels built a nest in the wiring, so the controls between the dashboard and the engine had to be rewired. The gas gauge for the aft tank always reads one-third, even when there's nothing left in the tank but an oily rainbow. There is radar, but it can be trusted only in full sun on a clear day. We trusted the Global Positioning System until the year it routed us from point A to point B on a straight course through an island. Following that course, we would have gouged across a beach, skidded up a mountain, and shot over a hemlock forest into a bay choked with rotten logs.

I'll grant that the boat has some virtues. Twenty-two feet long, with a thunderous 200 HP engine, it's fast enough to get us past the scary parts, the open ocean crossings, before the weather changes. It's big enough to carry us and all our gear, including little boats; but it's small enough to trailer from home to port—if we don't mind that on the worst bumps the bouncing trailer lifts the car and sets it down pointed in unpredictable directions.

"It gets us where we want to go," Frank says in ETHEL's defense.

"So far," I point out. But I'll say this: When we pull safely into the dark calm water at Pine Island—say it's evening and the crossing was wretched and windy—I love the huge pool of silence the rumbling engine creates when it finally clanks, shrugs, and stills. I love the way the boat gives under my weight when I move across the deck, as if it were water itself, and the smell of gasoline fumes mixing with hemlock and salt wind. I love the way the boat holds its anchor while the tide flows past, raising a little bow wave and piling kelp against the anchor lines, and how safe I feel, anchored by strong ropes. I can walk onto the bow sprit as if it were a diving board and when I look down, there is the ocean under my rubber boots, and clear jellyfish soggering past the starboard bow.

In this bay, the tide drops an average of fifteen vertical feet twice every day. At low tide, the island is a heap of trees and ferns on a bastion of rock. Between the forest and the sea is a long, sharply sloping jumble of waist-high boulders slippery with sea anemones. So we off-load ETHEL at high tide, when we can nose the bow into the grasses just below camp. Then we anchor the boat offshore, away from the rocks, where it safely rides the rising and falling tides.

To get between ETHEL and the island, we launch two little boats off ETHEL's stern—Professor Plum, my tiny purple kayak, and the Valdez, a blue fiberglass boat about the size and shape of a single bed. I call this boat the Valdez because it's a disaster waiting to happen. The big problem is how to anchor Valdez and the Professor. On an island with a fifteen-foot tide, you can't just tie a little boat to a tree and expect to row away in the morning, because in the morning, the boat will lie all aslant on broken rocks, a long, slippery way to the water. If you tie up at low tide, wrapping the line around a rock, the rising tide will either sink your boat or unwrap your line and carry the boat to the end of the bay, depending on how good you are at tying knots.

To solve that problem, we stretch a loop of rope on pulleys across a little bay indented in the island and tie the boats' painters to the rope. When we want a boat, we walk to the edge of the water and pull the rope in, hand over hand, as if it were a tenement clothesline.

I love this, the early morning in dense fog, when all I can see is a skim of silver on the water—no trees, no island, no boats. I climb down wet rocks to the edge of the bay and haul on the rope. The pulleys squeak and I can hear the boats knock against each other and thump on rocks. In time, the bow of the little purple kayak noses through the fog, glistening with dew. I pull it to shore, unhook the line, lower myself into the inevitable puddle on the seat, paddle softly, and disappear into the fog. The people I love will be lying in warm sleeping bags, listening for the lap of my paddle on the water, but all they will hear are red-throated loons yipping like coyotes some-where off in the whiteness, and a raven, muttering to himself. I love this.

In fact, for all its unfriendly weather and indifferent algae, the island is a place all the members of my family are deeply attached to, a place where we embrace each other, coming from far away to rejoice at the chance to stand together in the rain. I'm trying to understand the oddity of this attraction. But the fact remains that when I remember images from all our trips to the island, they are—as often as not—images of love. Well, rain. But also love.

IN YELLOW RAINGEAR and hip boots, our son, Jonathan, and Anne, who will soon be our daughter-in-law, stood knee-deep in Dead Bear Bay. The day was terrible, even by southeast Alaskan standards—driving rain, a gray ceiling of clouds, and fog tearing in shreds from the water. But they seemed not to care about the weather, maybe because dense schools of salmon milled around in front of the stream, waiting for high tide. Erin and I were sitting under canvas in ETHEL, anchored in the bay, glad to be out of the weather. There were so many salmon, jumping so high, that from our vantage point, it looked like an underwater juggler was flinging fish into the air. Anne stood braced against the pull of a salmon, yellow-hooded face, yellow-slickered shoulders, boots planted in the gravel edge of the inlet.

Jon slogged out of the water and stood beside Anne, reaching down just now and then to raise her rod tip. The fish took a grand leap and the yellow shoulders flinched. Anne wound quickly, bending over the pole, and he stood beside her until the fish was almost to her feet, arcing its body and splashing side to side. Only then did Jon lean toward the water and lift the fish with both hands. One hand cradled the plump belly of the salmon, the other ringed the narrow place in front of its tail. He held it close to his chest, proudly and tenderly, as if the salmon were a baby in shining silver pajamas.

Jon lifted the fish into the Valdez, beached in the gravel. But the tide was coming in and the Valdez was starting to float. Taking the bowline in his hand, he pushed the boat into the water. Anne climbed in, swiping rain off the seat. The next time I looked in their direction, Anne was sitting in the little barge, reading a book. Rain poured onto her back and dripped off her hood. She had the book open inside a clear ziplock bag and periodically she pulled off her mitten and reached into the bag to turn the page. Jonathan stood in the bay, casting his line into a school of salmon. The tide was running fast, so he'd tied the boat's bowline to his belt, to keep Anne and her silvery salmon from drifting out to sea.

That night, back in camp, Frank dipped the shiny pink fillets in sesame oil and dropped them into a hot skillet. For a while, we couldn't hear the rain on the tarp, for all the noise of the snapping oil. In a few minutes— not too long—Frank slid the fillets onto plates. That night, Anne ate salmon she caught with her own hands, and I remember how desperately we all hoped she liked the taste of fish and rain and wildness.

❧

AT THE ISLAND, we are always tying knots. Tying boats to fixed anchor lines, tying gas cans into the boat, tying cord around trees to hold tarps or frying pans or water buckets, tying a rope to a crab pot. Tying a fish head inside a shrimp trap, threading wire through its eye socket, a horrible enough job, the gill plate sharp enough to slice your hand, the eye watching you work.

Frank loves knots. All his knots are clean and tight, all his ropes are coiled. At home, he watches a knot Web site that shows ropes rolling slowly into graceful loops and cinching themselves into complex knots. The free end hoists itself erect, pauses as if to look around, and then pushes deliberately through the loops.

For a week before we left for the island, Frank took rope to bed with him. I would be curled under the covers

with a book, and Frank would be lying stretched out on
his back in bed, holding up a short length of cord. In the
spotlight of his reading lamp, he formed the coils, then
pushed the free end through the loops, gently. When the
rope was perfectly entangled, he slowly pulled both ends,
and tied the knot. "Here," he said one night, rousing me
from that halfway place between reading and sleeping,
"I made you a monkey's fist," and he handed me a solid
ball of rope with an intricate pattern on the surface, like
a woven basket.

THERE IS A HIDDEN COVE at the end of the inlet,
accessible only two times a day, at slack high tide. That's
when the tide stops flowing and we can get a boat
through the narrow channel into the cove. When the
tide is running, the current creates a dangerous moving
waterfall, a tidal bore. But it's worth waiting for slack
tide. There are often bears patrolling the beach in the
secret cove, and nervous geese, and the site of a native
village from long ago. Glacier-gouged mountains rise
from the beach. And always on our minds is the cer-
tainty that if we misjudge the tides, we'll be stuck in the
cove as shadows rise up our backs, and we'll spend half
the night bobbing in the water while moisture settles
on our shoulders and something snorts in the salal on
the shore.

One day, Frank wanted to go into the cove to see if
there were salmon schooling in the mouth of the river.

But, impatient, he mis-timed the tide. The falls were buried, but the tide was still running; water swirled in violent gyres and currents, and lifted into standing waves where the tide collided with the water of the cove. The channel was too shallow for the big boat, so we piled into the Valdez, like five people riding a bed, Frank in the stern with his hand on the tiller of the outboard motor. He decided we would go through the narrows, and we would go through backwards.

Unless you're going faster than the current, or slower, you can't control the direction of a boat in moving water. You could point the bow in the direction of the current and gun it, but that's dangerous because you go too fast to avoid rocks or make the small adjustments you need for a tricky current. So you do what Frank decided to do. You point the boat into the current and plow upstream, but slowly, more slowly than the current flows, so that you gradually wash downstream to where you want to go.

As his passengers gripped the Valdez's gunwales and made hopeless little noises, Frank puttered upcurrent, responding to the eddies with minute adjustments on the tiller, turning into the flush of each whirlpool, flinching when a current slammed the boat. Slowly we lost ground and washed through the swirling narrows.

THIS FAR NORTH, darkness comes gradually and inconclusively. At dusk, soft, nasty blackflies come out, crawling across our foreheads to bite the places where our hats meet our heads. To avoid them, we often go to bed while it's still light, tucking into warm sleeping bags and zipping the mosquito net behind us. As a result, we seldom get to see the stars.

But on a night of the Perseid meteor showers, I was determined to see the stars. Frank wasn't so sure about this plan, but he set his watch alarm for 2 A.M. When it jarred us awake, we fumbled around for warm waterproof clothes and crawled out of the tent. We didn't turn on a flashlight because we didn't want to dim our night vision. Besides, we didn't have far to go because the tide was high, sloshing on the rocks a short, lumpy hike down the path from camp.

Frank and I stood by black water and looked up. The North Star was high in the sky, higher than we had ever seen it. Cygnus the swan, the great northern cross, had slipped toward the south; it glowed in a cloud of star-light at the portal of a spiral arm of the galaxy. Little meteors darted through the darkness—tiny incandescent traces that vanished as soon as we found them. When I stepped onto a rock underwater, bioluminescent plank-ton sparkled under my feet. Sharp pinpricks of light rode the rings my boots raised on the water. Tiny explosions flowed off my boots.

I shook the underwater rock wrack—a spray of sparks—then lifted cupped hands. Starlight swam in my palms and dripped between my fingers to the water, where it exploded and vanished. I threw a spray of sparks into the bay. What could be more wonderful? Stars above us, stars below, stars exploding in our hands. "You could create a universe this way," I said, "standing in the starry depths, slinging light into the night sky."

"God," Frank said, rubbing his forehead. "These bugs are awful."

I turned on him, fast as a falcon. "Just go, then. Go back to the tent. Leave me here."

There was a long silence as stars shot willy-nilly through space, and algae sparked against our boots.

"I can't," he finally said. "Because I love you, and if you skid into those 'starry depths,' I should be here to pull you out."

We stumbled through the darkness back to the tent. I had inhaled a blackfly, and I coughed a long time before I fell asleep.

🐝

THE NEXT DAY WAS our thirty-second wedding anniversary. I took a boat out to track down a soft, syncopated cry we'd been hearing through the fog, like this—ga-ga-guhGA, ga-ga-guhGA—and to think about love. I wanted to understand what it means to love a place. Clouds sat right on the water, so I couldn't see anything but white light. I was trying to be quiet so I didn't scare whatever was making that sound, but I'd brought the wrong boat, the Valdez with its loose and clanky oars. I shipped the oars and let the tide tangle me in a pile of kelp. My boots were jammed between the gas can and the anchor, my notebook was on my lap, and little pains fluttered like moths up and down the muscles of my back. The island is a place of lifting and pulling—hoisting anchors and crab pots and buckets of stream water in and out of boats, raising two hundred feet of wet rope and a loaded trap of shrimp.

In the Sea of Cortez, Jonathan studied the ecology of islands. He wanted to know how islands change the sea and how sea life shapes the shore, mice eating sea bass that wash up on shore, guano from frigate birds nourishing the algae greening around the island. He wanted to understand all the beautiful, complicated connections between land and sea that make life flourish over time, the complex patterns of interdependence and mutual sustenance. This is what I want to understand too—the beautiful, complicated ways that love for people is all mixed up with love for places. The ecology, one might say, of caring.

I opened my notebook. Let's put this gathered evidence in front of us and let it speak. Love has as its object: daughter, son, young woman who loves son, sudden quiet, a certain combination of smells (hemlock, saltwater, gas fumes), mist swimming with light, purple kayak, fogbound island, hidden cove, and a man who can drive a boat backward through a whirlpool. The list is, of course, incomplete. Add silver salmon. Add unexpected sun. Add the whirlpool.

I was trying to figure out the difference between loving a person and loving a place, but I wasn't making much progress. My son *is* this place, and each gravel shore and hidden halibut speaks of him. Is it any wonder that I love them both? And how can I distinguish between my daughter and the rain in her hair, this young woman who always stands in the bow of the boat, where wind flattens her raincoat against her body and dashes seawater over her face?

The fog had lifted and I found myself among tiny islands, each only one tree's worth of island. Each island had a rime of seaweed at its sea edge, yellow in the sudden sun, then a mound of bare gray rock and a single hemlock tree dragged down by clumps of moss and shredded lichen. The islands floated on their own reflections—not perfect, but cut into horizontal lines, minutely displaced. I threw a line over a branch and made myself fast—I didn't want to drift too far away—and then the reflections were spots of color, dancing.

I stretched my back and started two lists. What does it mean to love a person? What does it mean to love a place? Before long, I discovered I had made two copies of the same list. To love—a person and a place—means at least this:

One. To want to be near it, physically.

Number two. To want to know everything about it— its story, its moods, what it looks like by moonlight.

Number three. To rejoice in the fact of it.

Number four. To fear its loss, and grieve for its injuries.

Five. To protect it—fiercely, mindlessly, futilely, and maybe tragically, but to be helpless to do otherwise.

Six. To be transformed in its presence—lifted, lighter on your feet, transparent, open to everything beautiful and new.

Number seven. To want to be joined with it, taken in by it, lost in it.

Number eight. To want the best for it.

Number nine. Desperately.

Love is an anchor line, a rope on a pulley, a taut fly line, a spruce root, a route on a map, a father teaching his daughter to tie a bowline knot, eelgrass bent to the tide, and all of these—a complicated, changing web of relationships, taken together. It's not a choice, or a dream, or a romantic novel. It's a fact: an empirical fact about our biological existence. We are born into relationships with people and with places. We are born with the ability to create new relationships and tend to them. And we are born with a powerful longing for these relations. That complex connectedness nourishes and shapes us and gives us joy and purpose.

I knew there was something important missing from my list, but I was struggling to put it into words. Loving isn't just a state of being, it's a way of acting in the world. Love isn't a sort of bliss, it's a kind of work, sometimes hard, spirit-testing work. To love a person is to accept the responsibility to act lovingly toward him, to make his needs my own needs. To love a place is to care for it, to keep it healthy, to attend to its needs as if they were my own, because they are my own. Responsibility grows from love. It is the natural shape of caring.

Number ten, I wrote in my notebook. To love a person or a place is to accept moral responsibility for its well-being.

I turned the Valdez toward camp, tugging on those

stupid clanking oars, scattering the reflections, picturing my family gathering one by one to explore the bay as the tide fell. They would be stumbling over rocks and calling to each other: "Look, here, under the kelp, a purple starfish."

SHY AFFECTIONATE SF

FRANK IS A SELF-DESCRIBED "hard" scientist. He
studies chemicals in the brain—how desire actually
works in the cells, the little switches and locks. He listens to me talk about what it means to love a place, but
he says I can't just assume that people care about places.
He says I need data. "I'm a philosopher," I told him.
"Philosophers don't *do* data." But the fact is, I had been
conducting a study of sorts. For several months before
we left for the island, I read the love ads in the Saturday
paper. The secret, coded yearning, the SWFs and DMs
all ISO something—this interested me. I would never
have had the occasion or even the temptation to phone
the Lonesome Horseman, or send a photo to Teddy Bear,
or tell Endangered Species that I'm a rarity myself, but
I was curious. Love ads are a data bank of human nature
far more revealing than the Human Genome Project:
fifty people every week explaining who they are and what
they are looking for, in twenty-five words or less.

I kept a count of love ads in the *Corvallis Gazette-*

Times, tallying up what people were searching for. The data revealed that more people like "the outdoors" than any other thing. The typical SF, a LARGE & BEAUTIFUL momma, 31, who is shy and honest, likes the outdoors, movies, and walking on the beach (in that order). The typical SM is a VERY FIT MALE, who is very sensitive. He likes the outdoors, romance, and tattoos (again, in that order). In all, fully two-thirds of the SFs and SMs listed "the outdoors" first on their lists—a clear winner.

After the outdoors, the first runner-up was watching movies. Beaches and camping tied for third place. Walks and hikes came in fourth. Then came dancing and dinner, followed by romance. (Let us pause to notice how long it has taken to get to romance—sixth on the list, after all the outdoor sports). After romance, there was a three-way tie among cuddling, fishing, and country-western music (although none of the people who liked to cuddle also liked to fish), and one vote each for mountains, darkness, the blues, Harleys, hand-holding, friendship, and vampires. My research found no significant difference between men and women, except that three women liked sports, which are of no interest whatsoever to the men. So there it is. People like the outdoors best of all, they say, better even than sex.

Frank received these data with the mixed astonishment and chagrin that only a scientist can muster. "Kathy, this is *bad science.*" I know that; but that doesn't mean it isn't important. I don't want to claim that everybody loves the outdoors; I just want to point out that many people do, and to observe that love for place and love for people are mixed together in beautiful and mysterious ways. I know a woman who walked through an ancient cedar forest and fell helplessly in love—with the forest and with the man carrying her sandwich. And I have seen people search all their lives for what would make them happy and whole and never think to look outside the door— perpetual seekers, not sure what they are looking for, but endlessly searching, on the Internet, in catalogs, at the mall.

I don't know if the people who place love ads in my home-town newspaper are typical of people in general. For that matter, I don't know if Oregonians are representative of human beings. And who knows if the people are telling the truth; maybe they just *say* they like the outdoors because they think that will attract a particular sort of person. I'm not claiming that the connection between loving a person and loving a place is simple. I just think it's sig-nificant that—more often than not—when people have an opportunity to envision their unlived lives, to dream about starting over and doing it right this time, the out-doors is the setting for their dreams. Big-Hearted Bob and Chantilly Lace walking hand-in-hand at the edge of the sea: the raised pulse, the rhythmic waves, the crying gulls, the salty, exultant wind.

In 1984, Harvard entomologist E. O. Wilson advanced the biophilia hypothesis, arguing that human beings have an innate attraction to living things. This attraction makes sense from an evolutionary perspective. "To an extent still undervalued in philosophy and religion," he wrote, "our existence depends on this propensity, our spirit is woven from it, hope rises on its currents." I like this hypothesis. It explains a lot: When we wall ourselves off from the natural world's wild sources of comfort and belonging, don't we feel a self-destructive restlessness, like a single moth in a jar? And Wilson's hypothesis *is* hopeful: If humans naturally love the living things on this planet—all the burrowing, breathing, breeding biotic systems, the foundations of our very lives—then maybe we can find a way to act lovingly toward them.

This is why I was happy to present Frank with evidence consistent with the biophilia hypothesis and to suggest one more thing. We are attracted to the great green earth—and to pink algae, blue fish, gasping newborn babies, and suction-cup tadpoles. But read the love ads closely and literally: ISO LTR. In search of a long-term relationship. The people who place ads in my hometown newspaper aren't just advertising for partners, they are advertising for love. Like all of us, what they seek is lasting relationship—with people and the planet—and what they cherish is relatedness, being in caring connection with a person or place. We are creatures who are born to love. It's more than biophilia that drives us. It's philophilia—the love of love itself.

REFRIGERATOR FUNGUS

KAYAKING BETWEEN ISLANDS, Jonathan and I came across a rock splashed with bright orange lichen. It was the sunburst lichen, a nitrogen-loving plant. Animal urine is full of nitrogen, so the presence of the lichen told us that some animal—a deer mouse maybe—liked to sit exactly there. "Makes me think of Grandpa," Jonathan said, and that's exactly what I was thinking. Jon climbed the cliff to look for a burrow, while I rocked in the boat, almost swamped by thoughts of my father. The first sight of those lichens, and he would have been digging under his raincoat for his hand lens and flopping on his stomach to get a closer look. A botanist and a teacher, he was fascinated by every living thing, but he had a special place in his heart for the agents of decay.

My father didn't get to Pine Island before he died, which I regret every day. At the island, he wouldn't have known where to turn first—the old man's beard dripping from every branch, the mold at the edge of a woodpecker's hole, decaying cedar stumps blooming into gardens of huckleberry, salal, deer fern, and the tiny red-capped lichen he called "Canadian Soldiers."

He thought bread mold was gorgeous, the infinitely many shades of green and blue. All through my child-hood, petri dishes sat stacked beside the leftover pot roast in the back of our refrigerator, growing bacterial cultures for my father's class or experiment. I remember that he once drew our initials with bacteria, dipping a stylus in a culture, then drawing it carefully across sterile agar in a petri dish. In a few days, he had three beds of agar monogrammed for his three daughters—*N, K,* and *S.* It made us feel special, our initials appearing slowly, just a few specks at first, then a line of brown spots bub-bling up fuzzy and fetid, eventually sprawling out and disappearing in a mottled, furry field.

He was a great fan of slime molds too. They are an oddity—not plant, not animal, but more primitive and surely more spectacular, cherry-red or raincoat-yellow slime that grows on decomposing wood. He would leave a slime mold on a plate at night, and by morning it would have crept onto the kitchen counter, head-ing—who knows where?—to the Cheerios box or back to the dark forest and moldering autumn banks.

It didn't matter if he was in the wilderness, in town, or in the basement brushing away spiderwebs—he would find some natural miracle to delight in. Walking beside a pasture at the edge of my hometown years ago, he noticed that all the cow pies had grown pelts of mold during the night. It was as if a hundred opossums had gathered in the field for a moonlit cocktail party, he said, and drinking too much, staggered and fell where they stood—a field of opossums, sleeping it off at dawn.

Small things always caught his attention, things most of us would overlook. He lay in ditches for hours, photographing a cicada as it emerged from the earth, or a dung beetle. Passing cars would screech to a stop and the occupants would pile out, sure they had discovered a corpse. Before long everybody would be on their stomachs, watching beetles mate tail-to-tail, while my sisters and I sat in the grass, dying of embarrassment. Over time, my father accumulated boxes and boxes of color slides, all carefully identified by their correct Latin names. *Xanthoria elegans*—that's the nitrogen-loving lichen.

When he was much older and retired from teaching, he started putting his slides together into shows. He chose a theme, selected slides, wrote a script, and then painstakingly choreographed the whole performance to music that he chose with the greatest care. He took the shows on the road, playing to retirement villages, schools, and church study groups.

When he died, the slide shows went into my attic in boxes stacked five feet high, carefully labeled. Inside each box was a carousel of slides, a script, and an audiotape of my father speaking over the music he had selected. For several years, I didn't have the courage to listen. But then I ran into a woman who'd been my father's friend. "He had such a nice voice," she said. "I loved to hear him speak." With that, I missed my father's voice more than anything in the world. So I dragged the boxes out of the attic, hooked up his old carousel projector and a tape player, and sat down to listen.

The day was dark enough for color slides, even with the curtains open. A November storm threw rain like stones against the window and tossed around the branches of a Douglas-fir, hurling green cones to the ground. I pointed the slide projector to the white wall and dropped a cassette into the tape player.

The first show featured a tour of Oregon—three-year-old Erin sitting in a puddle, a gorgeous panorama of Crater Lake. "The explosion that formed Crater Lake blew rocks the size of grand pianos all the way to Canada." Then I watched a sequence of photographs called *Home Life of the Mourning Dove*. It peered in on a family of mourning doves raising their babies to the tune of Beethoven's Sixth Symphony, the organ with its joyous right hand. My father had taken all the pictures into a mirror angled over the nest so he wouldn't disturb the birds on their "slapdash wisp of a nest." Another show was about metamorphosis—frogs, caterpillars, and children, my grandmother and Ecclesiastes, a time for every purpose. Then *This Land I Love*—mountain thunderstorms, Woody Guthrie, and railroad tracks silver in the rain.

The next slide show took me back to a darkened room. My father is an old man, a widower, full of cancer, but he is still sturdy and his voice is firm and rich. His audience is a group of elderly people at the Elyria, Ohio, Senior Center. Though the title of the program is *The*

Cycle of Life, there is no denying that the subject really is decay. Here is a soft-focus photo of small mushrooms, *Marasmius rotula,* growing on a decomposing leaf.

"The old leaf surrenders the atoms that furnish the substance of its life," he explains, "returning these atoms to the stream of living things from which they were borrowed. No living thing has a permanent claim upon its atoms."

His voice is deep—a preacher's voice, though he was a professor—and deeply respectful, as if he were reading the Bible. The pitch of his voice drops at the end of every phrase. I can't help but wonder what his audience is thinking about all this rot and decay, as music from a pan flute softly floats in the background.

"The cycle is pushed along by agents of decay that keep the cycle going. Like it or not, most life on earth would end without them: the ubiquitous molds . . ."

And now it is the swelling sounds of the Mormon Tabernacle Choir and full orchestra, Bach's Cantata no. 208, *Sheep May Safely Graze.*

". . . and bacteria that take nitrogen from the air and put it in the soil. The slime molds . . ."

Trumpets join the soaring soprano voices.

"All of these keep our earth from being one great graveyard."

And here is a picture of a lipstick-red slime mold, *Tubifera ferruginosa,* all lumpy and slimy on a decomposing stick.

"What a marvel. What a marvel that these simple atoms can be arranged in so many ways, giving life to so many kinds of plants and animals . . ."

Close focus on a hamster. A mandrill. An iguana.

"... and even a little girl." I am startled to be looking at a picture of myself, maybe five years old, sitting on my father's lap with my head leaning against his shoulder. The music swells, his voice slows and deepens. "What a wonder that these atoms, arranged so precisely, provide a body able to carry on all the functions of life:

even to wonder,

and laugh,

and sing,

and cry,

and die."

Massed choirs and orchestra, the singing brass, a glorious fullness of sound.

The music faded away and the show was over. I punched off the tape player and rested my head on my arms.

❦

JONATHAN HAD CLIMBED beyond the nitrophilous lichen and sat perched on a storm-polished log. He was intently watching mew gulls as they circled over the beach, crying like newborn babies. They lifted purple sea urchins high into the air, dropped them on the rocks, and swooped down to pick the flesh between cracked prickly plates. I lifted my binoculars to watch the gulls, but put them down again, still caught up in memories of my father.

On that stormy November afternoon, I had opened a box of my father's slides labeled *Wonder*. The slides were

there, tidy in their carousel. But the script was missing
and there was no tape. I clicked the carousel into the
slide projector. A red leaf against the bright blue sky. A
Polyphemus moth laying eggs on the blue velvet chair in
my father's living room. A close-up of some sort of mold,
like skinny lightbulbs with black caps. My mother and
her baby grandson, all cheeks and soft skin. Watermelon
snow, the pink algae that grow on snowdrifts. I checked
the box again for a script or tape I might have overlooked.

Of all the things I could have lost, I had lost my father
on the subject of wonder. The click and whir of each falling slide dropped into a silence that unsettled me. What
was he saying about a red leaf in a blue sky? What is the
meaning of snow that turns pink in the sun? What did it
mean to him—his grandson in his wife's arms? And what
music did he choose? What is the background music for
wonder?

As color pictures silently shifted and blinked on
the wall, black walnuts dropped with a clunk from my
neighbor's tree onto the pavement. Rainwater gurgled
through the gutter by the window, rushed down the
drainpipe, and rivered into the heaped-up walnut leaves.
Through rain-slicked piles of leaves, cars whirred down
the street, running over the nuts. The shells cracked open
with a sharp report. Crows tumbled down cawing to pick
at the nut meats, then flapped and carred on the telephone line.

The broad face of a short-eared owl filled the screen,
and it suddenly occurred to me that maybe there never
was an audiotape crammed with words and music.
Maybe wonder falls silent. Maybe wonder is just this: the

silence of a human being, come face-to-face at the end of his life with a world of unspeakable mystery and beauty. Astonishment beyond words. Gratitude beyond expression. And what could the music of wonder be to a man who is about to die, but the sound of this stream of living things? That's what my father called it—the stream of living things.

✸

ROCKING IN MY KAYAK, I watched my son perched at the crest of the island. His attention had been caught by something far out to sea. His binoculars rested useless on the seat of the kayak, but he was standing now, looking intently toward the west. He raised his arm and pointed. I turned my binoculars to that place. It was a pod of dolphins, silver curves jumping in unison, shining just for a moment, then sliding into the sea.

I believe that the most loving thing you can say to a person is "Look." And the most loving stance is not a close embrace, but two people standing side by side, looking out together on the world. When people learn to look, they begin to see, really see. When they begin to see, they begin to care. And caring is the portal into the moral world.

"Look, there, almost to the edge of the sea. Can you see them?"

Jonathan pointed to a far place on the horizon where light leapt and leapt again.

LATE AT NIGHT, LISTENING

ONE NIGHT AFTER DINNER, Erin and I strapped on
headlamps, pulled on high boots, stuffed an extra flashlight in each pocket, and stepped out of the yellow circle
of lantern light into the dark, heading to the cove. It
was the night of the lowest tide of the month. On a tide
that low, the mossy edge of the island hangs precari-
ously eighteen feet over the water on a pedestal of rocks.
Slicked with algae, concealed sometimes by sea lettuce
or shiny sheets of winged kelp, the rocks are treacher-
ous enough in daylight. In the dark, we lowered ourselves
crablike, wedging our boots into cracks, our headlamps
shooting wildly into the trees across the cove.

At the edge of the water, we followed narrow beams
of light through the strange land that appears and disappears with the phases of the moon, slowly rising from
black water and sinking away by morning. We moved
carefully, testing each footstep, staying so close together
we bumped shoulders. Hermit crabs scurried out of the
way. Under an overhanging rock, our headlamps spotlighted a colony of orange-striped globules dripping

mucus and algae in threads to the water. Pink-striped anemones hung from thick stalks, heavy under their own weight. They shuddered when we touched them, and so did we. Orange worms hung from curling tubes, their own weight lengthening them into glistening threads. Wherever we looked, flat slabs of kelp shone in lamp-light. Chitons, polished like leather, stuck fast to rock. There were acorn barnacles as big as fists, barnacles on the barnacles, and leaf barnacles with fleshy necks.

We looked around for a place to sit—not easy in the intertidal zone. Sit on barnacles, and they'll prick holes in your rainpants. Sit on kelp, and you're likely to skid off into the drink. We found some patches of rock wrack for an uneasy perch and turned off our lights.

Sea smell rose around us, salty and thick. In the dark, we listened intently. At first, all we heard was the sea itself, the soft inhale, the asthmatic, gurgling exhale. Then gradually, spaces between the rocks began to tick and pop. Seaweed squeaked. Scritching moved in around us—tiny claws and bubbling jaws behind us, to our sides. There was a constant plop plop as saltwater dripped off invisible globules and bobules and tentacles and god knows what else. The loudest sound was a steady tick by my right hand, but then something big breached the water and slapped back down. I heard Erin suck in her breath. Water lapped against the shore. There was a flurry of scritching and a long sigh.

I shifted on my slippery perch, startling the whole world into silence. Erin switched on her headlamp and scanned the water.

"Eyes," she announced.

"Dozens of eyes."

Startled, I stared into the water. Nothing but darkness.

"No, hundreds," she said, swinging her headlamp beam across the bay. "Hundreds of them. Little yellow eyes. Like tiny cats around a campfire."

I searched the black water.

"Turn on your headlamp," Erin commanded, standing up. I flicked the switch, and there they were, staring back at me, pairs of tiny yellow eyes—wary, watching eyes.

I reached into a pocket for a flashlight. There is a limit to how much darkness a person can tolerate at the edge of black water.

The light searched through an underwater world that suddenly appeared, like a green-lighted tunnel through black mountains. Down through the water, I could see sea lettuce lifting. Periwinkles spiraling solid against rock. A village of barnacles in a forest of tube worms, with pink palm leaves waving overhead. A fat-headed sculpin fanning lacy fins so closely matched to the sand that they looked like currents stirring the water. Then my light found a pair of little shining eyeballs. The eyeballs bobbled at the base of long, waving antennae, as ephemeral as dotted lines, and the antennae sprouted from the head of a shrimp. There they were, standing on their tiptoes on gravel, little bent cylinders of pink-striped skin around clear water, with beaded legs no thicker than whiskers— hundreds of shrimp, all turned toward us, staring into our lights.

Up in the clean tree-and-rain world, Frank and Jon were leaning over their work, tying salmon flies, unaware of all this gooey flesh, all the striving and scrambling, all these little prickling awarenesses. Erin and I, too: we'd been living our daylight lives on the surface of the island, thinking we were alone out here, if we thought about it at all, thinking we were in charge, never dreaming of the other worlds that come out at night.

"God, I wish René Descartes were here," I said.

Erin laughed; she's used to this. But it was true. Enlightenment philosophers have mapped out such a miserable, lonely world for us to live in. For three, four hundred years, we children of the Enlightenment have sat alone and damp-eyed in a world of nothing but stone and dumb brutes, the only spirit in a universe of matter and mechanical animal-clocks, the only shining eyes in a universe stripped of mystery, exposed to human understanding and control, reduced to human convenience. Lonely kings of the stony mountain, we warily watch the world through our weak and narrow beams of light, denying the existence of everything we can't see clearly and distinctly, the unimagined other worlds watching us in the dark. I wish Descartes would plunk right down here on a slimy rock.

"It's slipperier than you think," I would warn him. He probably would struggle to move around the kelp bed in his long woolen robes—Frank would have to lend him boots—and I know he wouldn't understand my high-school French. But I would clear off a slithery cascade of kelp and point insistently to a rock. Accustomed to moving by candlelight, he might surprise me with how comfortably he finds his way in the dark.

"Here," I would say, grabbing his hand. "Stick your finger into this anemone and feel it shrink away from you. Reach into the water. Try to touch those waving tentacles at the mouth of the tube. See them snap away? Reach out to touch the sculpin; look how it disappears in a puff of sand. Turn off your headlamp. All the eyes will vanish. Move once, just wave an arm, and every sound will stop. And you'll be sitting in a world that is *froid, sombre, muet, et vide.*" Maybe he'd look up startled. "And you, doubting the truth of anything you can't clearly and distinctly perceive, will believe that the world is in fact, cold, dark, silent, and empty.

"But if you sit still in the dark, breathing quietly, the world will come to life around you. Astonishment will rise in you like the slow tide, sliding in under the soles of your feet. And then you will understand: you are kin in a family of living things, aware in a world of awareness, alive in a world of lives, breathing as the shrimp breathe, as the kelp breathes, as the water breathes, as the alders breathe, the slow in and out. Except for argon and some nitrogen, every gas that enters your lungs was created by some living creature—oxygen by plankton, carbon dioxide by the hemlocks. Every breath you take weaves you into the fabric of life."

He probably wouldn't understand a word I said.

By then, dampness had seeped through my rainpants, through my fleece pants, into my polypropylene long underwear. This is not good. Clothes dampened by rain or dew will dry again. But once clothes are soaked with seawater, the salt will pull water toward itself incessantly, and the clothes will be irredeemably soggy.

"Ready to go back?" I asked Erin, and we crawled on hands and boots up the slippery rock, like bears, pulling ourselves gingerly over barnacles, until the sharp smell of the sea gave way to the must of ancient cedar duff, telling us we were close to a sip of brandy and a warm sleeping bag.

I'M ONE OF THOSE people who never can think of the right words in the heat of the moment. All night I mulled over how complicated and layered and open-ended this kinship of humans with all of natural creation actually is, this beautiful, bewildering family.

First, there is the kinship of common substance. Like a sea slug or a horse-neck clam, I am carbon atoms spun through time, arranged and rearranged in patterns. Break my pattern down to atoms, and I can scarcely be distinguished from the stars. Second, there is the kinship of common origins. The gooseflesh that prickles my skin is what's left of the contraction that bristles the fur of a frightened bear and fluffs a bird in February. Third, there is the kinship of interdependence. Consider the sweet-rotting hemlocks that create vanillin, which nourishes the mycophylae, which produce fruiting bodies, which feed the flying squirrels, which nourish the spotted owls, which entrance a middle-aged woman, who warms the rotting tree with her fleece bottom. And fourth, the kinship of a common fate. We, all of us—blue-green algae, galaxies, and bear grass, philosophers and clams—will some day dissipate into vibrating motes. In the end, all of natural creation is only sound and silence moving through space and time, like music.

The same arguments get trotted out, over and over again, in a dogged effort to preserve a place on the pedestal for humans alone. Here's the old favorite: It would seem that humans are apart from and above the rest of natural creation, for the Bible says that God created man in his own image, several days after he created the birds of the air and the fish of the sea, and gave man dominion over all the creatures that walk and fly and swim.

But I would say it's only arrogance that makes humans think that because God made us last he must have made us best. Why couldn't people as readily believe that by the time God got around to making people he had run out of ideas, so he did a little recycling. The same systems that propel giant squid through the seas move blood through our hearts, and our cells use the same notation that directs the growth of red rock crabs. We breathe the same oxygen as the fish of the sea and the birds of the air, and it turns to the same carbon dioxide in our lungs. To make our minds, our exalted minds, God blew into the brain of a lizard. Our great temples have the proportions of a snail.

If we truly are made in the image of God, then God, too, must be made of the stuff of lizards, or lizards are made of the stuff of God. We should rejoice in every human being, and every squid and sculpin—the progenitors of what is divine in us.

A different argument comes from Descartes. Humans have minds, or consciousness, he wrote, "the thinking substance." But plants and animals do not. So humans are apart from and superior to plants and animals.

The fact is, I don't know for sure what animals are thinking, but neither did Descartes, and that seems like a good reason not to rush to judgment about what's on an animal's mind. How suspiciously convenient it is to believe that humans have the monopoly of the universe on mind. If people are going to imprison dolphins and transmogrify the gall bladders of bears into fortifying elixirs, if they are going to scrape the bottom of the ocean bare and grind the hindquarters of black-tailed deer into patties, if they are going to reduce owl nesting sites to toilet paper and convince themselves that this is not a problem, then they will need to believe that humans have minds but other animals do not. But this is a matter of convenience, not truth.

Awareness remains the great mystery, unexplained, maybe unexplainable. Which one of us can explain what happens in our own bodies to transform quanta of energy into an awareness of starlight reflected on water? Who knows what happens in a human's mind as she watches that star lift, flare, and tangle in floating kelp— that gladness, that wanting more. And then who could claim to know what happens behind the seeing eye of a shrimp?

Every time we stab our narrow focused beams of light into the darkness we find another astonishing world, never imagined. All around us, animals cry out, and wince, and leap, and stare with their bottomless eyes. What pitifully limited imagination would convince us, time after time, that what we see is all there is—that because we cannot plumb them, there are no depths?

Then there's a last argument. I don't know if there's a person left on the planet who would defend this argument in public, but I also don't know if there's anyone who doesn't believe it deep down, or hope it's valid. Here it is: Humans can alter the other parts of creation and remain unaltered themselves. Therefore, they must not be part of an interdependent whole.

This is the saddest, most self-destructive mistake of all our sad and self-destructive mistakes, to think that humans can degrade their habitats and not degrade themselves. Counterevidence engulfs us—in epidemics of asthma in smoky cities, in lead-poisoned children, in Tlingit stories about the lost salmon, in broken families and dysfunctional cities, in landslides and vacant streams.

"You could cut off my hand, and I would still live," Powhatan-Ren'pe writer Jack Forbes told me. "You could take out my eyes, and I would still live. Cut off my ears, my nose, cut off my legs, and I could still live. But take away the air, and I die. Take away the sun, and I die. Take away the plants and the animals, and I die. So why would

I think my body is more a part of me than the sun and the earth?"

When I sit in the dark and listen, this is what I hear: Seawater drips from sea palms. Rain ticks through hemlocks. A man and his son murmur in lantern light. A winter wren startles from sleep. A kelp crab shuffles under sugar kelp. A boat creaks in the pull of the tide. It's all one symphony—all the small songs sounding in the darkness, coming together to create one beautiful night. Whatever harm we do to any part of the music, we do to the harmony of the whole. The discordance we create will be in our lives and the lives of our children.

RAVENS WERE CALLING early the next morning. I rolled over in my sleeping bag and zipped open the tent. Between hemlocks, I could see seawater tucked up tight to the edges of the island. The fleshy dark caverns, the kelp forests felled by their own weight, the entire creeping, slithering world was gone. If I didn't know better, I could believe it had never existed. In its place was bright, silent light and the silhouette of a loon, floating on the glare.

TOWARD AN ECOLOGICAL
ETHIC OF CARE

Preservation of a web of relationships is the
starting premise of an ethic of care.
—Joan C. Tonto, *Signs*

WE'RE DRENCHED IN SILENCE on Pine Island—or not silence exactly, but sounds that space themselves out over time, as distinct as islands in a river. A kingfisher chitters. An anchor chain rattles over a gunwale. A red-throated loon quacks like Daffy Duck. Maybe an outboard motor hums just at the edge of hearing, as Frank brings the Valdez in from a halibut hole. Between these small sounds are long expanses of time when all we can hear is the rustle of time's river, like wind sweeping past our ears.

So when a bald eagle winged by me on ETHEL's deck, I could hear every feather rasp against the wind. Part of me could have stayed forever in that peace. But I'd paddled out to ETHEL because suddenly, and for no reason I could figure, I wanted to talk to my sister. Funny how I work so hard to get to the wilderness, but as soon as I escape humanity, I start thinking about my family, and after a couple of weeks, I'm wrestling with the two-way radio, trying to call home.

I clicked on the radio and adjusted the squeal. When atmospheric conditions are right, a marine operator can sometimes splice a call through. There was a burst of static and a man's incomprehensible question. "5 1 0," I began, hoping without evidence that the voice had asked for a telephone number. A sea lion watched me blankly—and honestly, the number talk made no sense to me either. But then I heard my sister's voice, drowning in static.

"We're not here to take your call. If you would like to leave a message, please press one."

But I didn't have any buttons to press. Alone with my family in the wilderness, I had no number one button to press. I stood helpless on deck, overwhelmed by the absence of my sister. I climbed over the stern into my kayak and paddled back to camp.

After I'd tied my boat, I climbed onto rocks to watch the sun go down. Silhouetted against a vaguely lavender sky, Erin and Jonathan wandered on the tidal flat below me. Clams squirted geysers of seawater into the yellow light that washed under the clouds. A flock of Barrow's goldeneye whistled into the bay, crash-landing feet first. Erin and Jonathan leaned over the tide pools, seeing what they could see, lifting blades of kelp to look for crabs. Then they straightened and stood together, looking toward the water as a seal moved quietly across the channel, pulling a wake of light. I like being here with my family, watching our children be suddenly brother and sister again after months apart.

This kind of kinship, this kind of caring, is important and good. Human beings are creatures who are drawn to one another. We humans are born into networks of dependencies and complications, hidden connections, memories and yearnings, births and rebirths, fierce, mysterious love—a web of relationships. Unless something goes terribly wrong, we know what it means to be cared for, and we know what it means to care.

How desperately we value these webs of relationship. Even the tiniest babies will search the nursery for a human face, seeking out the embrace that brings them comfort and sustains their lives. As we grow older and grow also as moral beings, we recognize broader and broader webs of relatedness, a larger family that extends even to strangers in faraway places. This sense of belonging can bring us comfort, and when we find ourselves alone and apart, we sometimes feel a sadness that edges toward despair. These are facts of the greatest moral importance: If we value caring relations, then it makes sense that we commit ourselves to act in ways that strengthen and reweave and sustain the webs of relationships that we value.

This has been the central argument of what philosophers call the "ethic of care"—one of the twentieth century's most important contributions to moral theory. It tells us that we ought to act in ways that preserve the webs of human relationships we cherish and depend on. Not from a sense of abstract duty, loyalty to a set of principles that force us, against our inclinations, to care. Not from a calculation that caring will increase happiness in the long run. But because we naturally care—how can we not? And, cherishing caring relationships, we bend our efforts to nourishing and protecting them.

If this is so, then to know what is right in any given situation requires a deep understanding of what makes mutually sustaining connections flourish in particular settings. Right acting requires an understanding of the ecology—one might say—of caring.

I'd been standing still so long that the turban shells and periwinkles around my boots had grown red antennae and hairy, blue-tipped legs. In the evening quiet, I could hear them tiptoe away, tapping tentatively over the stones— the rustle of hermit crabs, soft, like the beginning of rain. The tide was slipping in, silver now under the purple sky, herding Erin and Jonathan back toward camp. Bending so close their foreheads almost touched, they leaned down to tuck their pant legs into their boots.

I think the ethic of care isn't only about relationships among people. After all, we're born into relationships, not just with human beings, but with the land—the beautiful, complicated web of sustaining connections that Aldo Leopold calls the "biotic community." Don't I value also my connections to the natural world—the deep biological connections that create and sustain me, the emotional connections that root me to land and anchor me at sea? And doesn't this kinship have moral consequences too?

"All ethics so far evolved," Leopold wrote, "rest upon a single premise: that the individual is a member of a community of interdependent parts," a community that includes "soils, waters, plants, and animals, or collectively: the land." We humans value our connections to the natural places that create and sustain us. The sudden awareness of kinship to the earth fills us with joy, and when we find ourselves away from the places we love, we're sadder, somehow reduced.

This web of emotional and biological relationships calls for acts of commitment. Right ways of acting are those that nurture, enhance, and celebrate healthy webs of connection among all the members of the biotic community. "Sing our love for and obligation to" the land, Leopold advised, and it's important to notice how quickly obligation follows on the heels of love.

I'm moved by the way the ethic of care and Leopold's land ethic lean toward each other, both gleaning moral wisdom from the human experience of loving and being loved. Both ethics respond to the sadness of separation, the disquiet people feel to be dangerously or unhappily apart—whether the separation is from families and communities, or landscapes and ecosystems.

I think the ethic of care has it right: The care we feel for people is the ground of our moral responsibilities toward them. And I think Aldo Leopold has it right: Our moral responsibility to care for the land grows from our love for the land and from the intricate, life-giving relationships between people and their places.

Then doesn't this follow?—that our moral calling must be to reknit and cherish healthy webs of connection not only to people, or not only to land, but also to families, human communities, landscapes, and biotic communities—all our relations.

What we need next is a new ethic—call it an "ecological ethic of care," call it a "moral ecology." It's an ethic built on caring for people *and* caring for places, and on the intricate and beautiful ways that love for places and love for people nurture each other and sustain us all.

I've never met Nel Noddings or any of the other people who first wrote about an ethic of care. But I once visited Leopold's farm in southern Wisconsin, the center of his writing life. Frank and I spent the night there after I'd spoken to a group of conservationists gathered under an old oak. The little cabin, a converted chicken coop they called the Shack, was the center of Leopold's family life, the place where the earth grew up into his children and grandchildren, as they replanted oaks and white pine and black-eyed Susans, tumbled into the Wisconsin River, swam at night in the great wash of sky over the Wisconsin prairie, and learned to care for the land as much as they cared for one another, although maybe it was hard to tell where one left off and the other began.

When the Leopold family stayed there, a slats-and-wire snow fence made a bed that stretched from one side of the little room to the other. No matter how many children were there, or how many friends, they all rolled up in blankets side by side on the fence, like logs in a woodpile. I could imagine teenagers sitting by a fire on the huge hearth in the morning, laughing or quarreling, and crowding around the little table lit by a kerosene lantern on a dim, rainy day. If anyone had walked by in the rain—which probably no one did, out there on the prairie—they would have seen a yellow glow from the rain-splattered windows, and heard the sound of laughter through the trees. They would have smelled wood smoke and wet pines.

Night was coming on. Erin and Jonathan had climbed back to camp; I could hear them digging into their dry bags for warmer clothes—an extra pair of socks, a wool hat. I dragged a kayak to the edge of the bay and paddled out to ETHEL. Climbing out of a kayak into a big boat is a tricky transition—you want to have a life jacket on. I jammed the bow of the kayak between the motor and the hull, reached up with two hands to grab the railing, and stood up in the kayak—a wobbly stance, probably stupid. Then, holding the kayak's bowline, I clambered on my hands and knees into the boat and turned on the two-way radio.

Occasionally when the weather changes—a shift in the wind, a flattening of clouds over water—we get a better connection to the outside world. But there was only static, spilling onto the silence of still water at dusk. I sat on the stern and watched a few gulls fly west, white against the shadowed forest. The last of the light had already left the snow on the mountains across the bay.

Sometimes I have a hard time at the end of a day. Something about the coming night, maybe, makes me lonely—or the dropping temperature, a certain shade of purple in the air.

LEAVING THE ISLAND

GALE WARNINGS. *Winds northwest 15 to 20 knots, easing to westerly, a few fog banks lowering visibility to near zero. Rain at times, increasing. Outlook: pressure 1005.2 and falling, winds west-northwest, rising to 25 knots. Seas 2 meters; combined seas 2.5 to 3 meters.*

The closer the time came for us to leave the island, the rougher the weather got. One or another of us was constantly checking the WX marine forecast, carrying the radio to the edge of the island for the best signal. The forecast was always the same — the same computer-generated voice, the same bad news.

Back in the curving channels, protected by mountains, only a light breeze prickled our little bay, so we couldn't feel the weather moving in. But we could hear it coming in the braying of seals on an island half a mile away: sounds get sharper and carry longer distances when weather lowers the clouds. We all knew that to get back to port, we had to somehow cross a broad arm of the sea fully exposed to the northwest wind. A wind can pick up a good head of steam across the reach of the north

Pacific. *Seas 2 meters:* that told us there was a big rolling ocean swell, with troughs six feet deep. *Combined seas 2.5 to 3 meters:* we could expect a steep, nasty chop on top of the swell.

We always leave ourselves some extra days because of the chance of bad weather, so we had some choices. We could stay on the island until the weather calmed or the wind changed direction. We would miss some appointments, worry friends. Fresh water we were okay on, because we could row to the creek. We wouldn't starve, because we could eat crab and shrimp. We'd need to save enough fuel to get out of here, so we'd have to be careful how many crabbing runs we made. Propane for the stove would be a problem, actually pretty soon, so it wasn't clear how we would cook our food. In all the summers we'd camped on the island, we'd never once built a fire, no matter how cold it got. We couldn't. Up here the wood is wringing wet—literally—about the consistency of liver. Raw fish from the sea?—probably okay. Raw shrimp? Well, none of this would kill us. And eventually the weather would let up.

That was option one, but marine forecasts predicted deteriorating weather in the next days, and even when the winds calmed down, it would take a day or two for the seas to settle. We were looking at a week, at least. That's a long time when it's pouring down rain and the whiskey's run out.

Option two? We could load up the boat and head to port. That's where our car and boat trailer waited for us, and restaurants and phones. Trouble wouldn't start until we left the chain of fjords and started south into the strait. That's five miles across and wide open to the wind, with nothing between there and Japan to damp the waves. If we made the crossing, we'd still have to run up the coast, and there are some big gaps between the islands that shelter that shore, and dreadful currents in a following sea. With this option, the chances of drowning could not be discounted. Actually, I wasn't sure that drowning mattered to me; fear would kill me long before waves washed over the stern and swamped the boat.

There was a third option. We spread the charts out on a rotting log and studied the branching network of fjords. What if we didn't head west out to sea? What if we loaded up the boat and headed inland instead? Our island is in the middle of a fjord that's part of a chain of flooded valleys that cut into the mountains of the mainland. If we chose a route up a channel that meets a dirt road, there was a chance that people would be camping or fishing there. If they were, there was a chance they would give us a ride to the highway, thirty-five rough miles, and then one of us could hitchhike to the seaport, pick up the rig, and drive back to load the boat.

The problem was, this venture would use up our boat gas, and if there was no one at the landing, or if the people there wouldn't help us, we'd be stuck. Unlikely we could use the radio back in the mountains. Clams we could always get, but August is a red tide month. Probably we could get crabs, certainly no shrimp. Probably flounder. But again, we'd be out of boat gas, low on stove fuel. We'd just have to wait for somebody to wander in. Frank studied the map. A freshwater stream flowed into the head of the fjord. A stream means spawning salmon at this time of year, and salmon often mean people.

Wind lifted the edge of the tarp and the pooled water spilled so hard and fast it overshot the yellow bucket we'd hung there to catch fresh water. The radio crackled. Gale warnings for tonight and tomorrow. Winds rising. We decided to wait another day.

Once I started to think about going home, home was all I wanted. It's like thirst; once you start thinking about it, you think you're going to die. It's so complicated, this relationship between wildness and home.

🌰

WE ALL HAD BINOCULARS out, scanning the shore for signs, as we motored east up a deep inland fjord toward what we hoped were people at the end of the road. Forested mountains rose straight from the sea on both sides of us, their peaks shiny with melting snow. Steep patches of timber had been clear-cut next to the water, but that was many years ago; already alders filled the scarp with light green foliage. Other than this, we saw no sign of human life. Waves rolled in under the stern, lifting and dropping the bow, so it was hard to hold binoculars. As we approached the end of the fjord, I thought I saw a glint between the trees, a car window maybe, but Erin was right: It could have been reflection on a waterfall or a wet rock. I scanned the beach; light splotches might be people, or piles of driftwood, or bears, I guessed, but there were definitely light splotches.

The boat bucked on down the channel. After a mile or so, the splotches turned into halibut carcasses—we could see them clearly now—huge halibut all filleted out to slabs as big as bath towels. Somebody had draped the carcasses over boulders on the beach. Bald eagles swarmed the halibut like gulls, tearing at long strips of intestines, or hunkered down on the beach, digesting. We lowered our binoculars and looked at each other: If there is a filleted fish, there is at least one fisherman holding a fillet knife. Not one of us said a word about luck.

We dropped anchor in deep water at the end of the bay, killed the engine, and took a vote. Who could most likely talk somebody into a ride? I lost. I was the most pitiful, my family decided, a middle-aged woman walking in rubber boots up the beach. They lowered a kayak for me, and I paddled in to shore.

There was, in fact, a trailer in the woods with a pickup truck parked beside it. I walked around the back, tres- passing uneasily. "Hello this place? Is anybody home?" The trailer was closed up tight. I knocked. Nothing. Stuff was left out everywhere—charcoal grill, thermos, bowls with chili still stuck to them, a dog's leash. They wouldn't have left food out in bear country if they didn't plan to be back before dark. So we had a chance—a chance for a ride down the dirt track to the highway, a chance that someone on the highway would stop for a hitchhiker in the dark, if anybody drove by.

But there was another pickup by the landing—a second chance. In a forest clearing between the gravel track and the bay, I found two young guys cleaning fish—sleeves rolled up, blood up to their elbows. I startled them; they must not have heard the boat come in. I told the long story. They listened. I asked for a ride.

"Nah," the tall one said. "We got a lot of halibut to clean."

"Here." He fished around in his pocket and threw me a set of keys.

"Just take the pickup."

†

WE DID. JONATHAN nosed ETHEL up to shore so Frank and Erin could jump off, then backed up the big boat and anchored in deep water where he and Anne would wait. Frank and Erin drove the long way round to town and picked up the car and boat trailer. That left me to sit on my kayak on the beach, thinking about human kindness. By nightfall, I heard Erin and Frank bumping down the road back to the cove.

I'd grown cold and tired of waiting, but I wasn't hungry. The family in the camper had come back, and without a word, a teenager walked down the beach and handed me a ham sandwich, an apple, a huge M&M cookie, and a can of Coke. I ate and drank it all, never thinking to save any for anybody else. You'd think, living

on an island, eating crab and shrimp and salmon fresh
out of the bay, that you'd never want anything else to eat.
But a ham sandwich—that was pretty good.

We stayed at a plywood motel that night. Got the
landlady out of bed to let us in. Ordered a carryout
pizza from a twenty-four hour place. Opened the windows to clear the old cigarette smoke. Called our family and friends. "Were there outhouses on the island?"
my sister wanted to know. "Did you have good weather?"
Through the window, we could see the boat sitting on its
trailer under a halogen lamp in the parking lot. Puddles
reflected oily rainbow light, and trucks roared by, raising
sheets of water against the hull.

AMAZING GRACE

DUSK AT MIDNIGHT. A long, slow dusk as the sun slides along the waterline, this night of the summer solstice. The ferry shakes, begins to grumble, and slowly moves past the breakwater that cradles the harbor town. I stand on deck with other people who don't mind rain or diesel fumes, our hoods cinched around our faces, moisture puddling in the folds, then overflowing down our cheeks. We're listening for whales — the gruff exhalation — and watching the seiners that pass on their way to port. Not much else is moving tonight. Just the ferry, shaking through the water between islands, and people adjusting the slopes of their hoods to keep rain out of their eyes.

In the boat's cabin, people are buying beer and choosing places by the windows, wiping the steam with their sleeves and bringing their faces close to peer through their reflections. Rain, furrowing down the glass, cuts their faces into wavy stripes, as if they'd been torn in lengths and imperfectly reassembled. As more lights come on in the cabin, people give up trying to see out and turn their attention to a young man tuning a guitar.

Another guitarist moves next to him, and they lean toward each other, listening with heads turned to one side, tuning their guitars together. I see them only vaguely through the windows, the bright raincoat colors running down the glass with the rain, and what I hear is not the wavering notes. What I hear is thrushes. Varied thrushes call and call, single sustained flute notes, blurred at the edges. But now and then, I hear a Swainson's thrush, a silky whistle spiraling from the forest, back where shadows have already arrived.

The boat churns on, curving between small islands. I watch closely, but no bears emerge from a cleft where a stream leaves the hemlocks. Snatches of song drift with cigarette smoke from the cabin. The guitar players are at that point where two strangers come together, probing for some sort of intersection, some song they have in common. Apparently there isn't much so far, because I hear songs that start out strong but end abruptly after a few phrases, then laughter. Or the guitarists take solo turns, gathering a few more people each time they happen on something they both can play and a few people can sing. From the forests, the Swainson's songs lift into the sky where, in a shield of deepest blue, a few stars are poking through.

I'm startled by the sky. The rain has let up and none of us even knew it, hunkered down in our hoods, sheltered under our own bowed heads, until we raised our eyes to the birdsong and found moonlight-rimmed clouds and the stars beyond. People fold back their

hoods, rubbing away hair that has plastered to their foreheads, and listen to sounds that are suddenly sharper and
easier to locate.

Cutting the engine, the boat coasts through a narrow channel and happens on a few scattered wanigans,
cedar-plank houses floating on logs chained to a shore
that rises in a sudden surge to mountains dusted with
snow. Most of the houses are dark and hard to make
out, but from one wanigan, a yellow window throws a
rectangle of light onto the bay. Someone on shore is
playing a wooden flute, a single line of music arriving
out of nowhere, one line of music on the expanse of dark
water between mountains. We recognize fragments of
"Amazing Grace," spiraling like the Swainson's thrush,
ziiing grace. The hidden flutist plays the notes again and
again, slowly, practicing—or maybe he's playing them in
simple celebration, *ziiing grace,* the downward cascade,
the upward sweep.

The people in the cabin must have heard the flute,
because now we hear the guitarists picking out the first
notes of "Amazing Grace," strumming experimentally
to get the right key for a new song, looking for a range
where people can sing. At first, people sing in unison,
and only a few know all the words. When the song is
over, the guitarists swing straight back to the first verse,
and this time people are surer of the words and the harmonies, and so they go on to stumble through the second verse. And over again, and over. The end of the song
becomes the beginning, and the harmonies deepen and
someone adds a descant, as the boat pushes through the

bay, pulling its wake past dark islands on a course that will take us into port.

The lights of a harbor town come into view around the black bulk of an island, a crescent of colored lights below the mountains, and the song cycles on. No one will let it end. I don't think there's a person left who's singing the melody line. Everyone is singing harmony and only the chords remain, the sustained density of all those voices singing different notes that somehow come together into something whole and beautiful and true, moving together through time and islands. We on the deck are singing too—not paying much attention to the words because the harmony itself has become the meaning of the song.

Amazing grace as the boat slides along the break-water, now only a blacker space in the black night. How sweet the sound as the bay reflects the lights of the little town—red and yellow and blue and white—and a crew-man stands in the bow, a black silhouette holding a rope in his hands. I once was blind, as the boat shudders to a stop and the crewman throws the rope to the dock, where a deckhand loops it over the stanchions. But now I see: the last of the wake washes over kelp-draped rocks and fades away, now, in the night, when the rain has stopped and moonlight outlines white clouds that rest on moun-tain peaks, when moonlight shines on the slippery dock, in this air that smells of low tide and creosote timbers, in the rippling town lights that reach out to us like music on the water.

AN ISLAND IN THE RIVER

near / far

Geography

The island in the Willamette River is an elongated mound of alluvial gravel carried by floods from the volcanic mountains of the Cascade Range. The river continually shapes and reshapes the island as water levels and velocity change. Floods pack material against the island's head—downed trees, sediments, sod torn from the bank—and transport gravel away from the tail. So the island migrates unsteadily upstream.

The stones making up the island are round and flattened. The force of the current flips the stones so that their edges point away from the current, stacking them in overlapping layers, like scales on a fish. From downstream, the armoring makes the island look rough; but from upstream, the island looks sleek and gray. Over time, the river removes and deposits gravel, replacing all the stones, but the island remains.

The island divides the current, which flows around both sides and curls into the tail. But some part of the river flows through the island, percolating between the stones. This water cools as it filters through the subsurface rocks, moderating temperature increases in the river. During low water, or in years when logjams block the channel, the island becomes part of the riverbank. But during regular flows, the shape of the island forces the current against the bank, digging and maintaining the channel that makes it an island.

There are many of these islands in the Willamette River, but this particular one adjoins a Corvallis, Oregon, city park and a complex of soccer fields, just upstream from the highway bypass bridge and the Evanite fiberglass factory, and just downstream of the water intake for the municipal water supply.

THIS IMPROVISATIONAL
HEART

IN WHAT TURNED OUT to be the last week of my
father's life, I flew to Ohio and found him sleeping in
his bedroom with the blinds drawn and the lights off.
No flowers, no Mozart or birdsong—just the bare room
in brown shadows. It startled me, this grim room, and
I blamed myself for staying away so long and leaving
his care to nurses. Without waking him, I went straight
into the backyard and cut armloads of apple blossoms
and lilacs and stuffed them overflowing into vases, filling his room with flowers. I tiptoed around, bringing
in a tape player and the music he loved, the triumphant
choruses. I put his alarm clock in a drawer—does a
dying man need to count time passing?—then opened
the curtains so light fell on the flowers, and raised the
windows to let in the smell of new-mown lawn. But
when my father woke up and looked around, he cried,
because he thought he was dead.

I didn't learn this until evening, and then I heard it from the nurses who had comforted him. They were nice about it, told me not to feel bad—how would I have known? But I should have known how to take care of my own father. Should have, but didn't. I stripped the room, putting his alarm clock back in exactly the same place, closed the blinds, and sat by my father in the dark.

Several years later, I was the one in the white crank-down bed, and it was my daughter who brought flowers to the hospital and sat by the bed, knitting a sock. Knitting, of all things; I could practically hear tumbrels rumbling down a cobblestone street. Chris was there too, her boyfriend, sitting in the corner, reading Homer. He kept popping up, looking at me, and plopping down again, like there was an electrical short in his chair. I felt fine, but I was 100 percent pissed off at my heart, which was skipping and bucking like a colt. This happens to me sometimes, is all. It's not dangerous, this incompetent heart, but I don't like when it acts up, and I was getting tired of waiting for the doctors to drug it into submission.

Hospitals are boring. I watched the line of the EKG leap and vibrate. A person could sing that line, I thought. Put it on a musical staff and it could be Stravinsky. I started to hum along, low tones on the flat places, but it was an awful song, thudding and buzzing, the "Flight of the Bumblebee" on dope.

The line traced a jagged horizon—the ridge of the Sierra de la Laguna in Mexico maybe—a volcanic land-scape in some raw and unpredictable place. Wherever it was, I wanted to go there. Imagine the lizards you could find in a landscape so busted up. Iguanas, I'm sure. Chuckwallas. We'd need to carry water. Wear hats. When our children were tiny, we hiked in the Cascade Range through an EKG landscape like that. The kids kept tripping, the rocks were so rough, and that hurt, falling with bare hands and knees on lava. So Frank and I took off our belts, looped a belt around the chest of each child, and held on to the tag end. Then, when the children tripped, we could lift them into the air before they hit the ground, and they were safe, flying over the cinders like angels on wires.

That first night in my father's house, the nurse had quietly opened the door to the room where I was sleeping. I saw her silhouetted in the slit of light. "What," I said suddenly, and sat up. "Your father can't sleep," she whispered. "He wonders if you could tell him a story, or sing to him."

A story? Sing? To my father? When I was a child, I knew how to love my parents; loving came naturally, like eating when you're hungry. When I was a parent, no one had to tell me how to love my daughter and my son. But this was something new, to be the mother to my father. I had never been at such a loss. So I sat by his bed and improvised.

I put my hand on his arm, as if I were trying to hold him down or something, and told him about how he once owned an electric lawn mower with a long extension cord, and how he ran the lawn mower over the cord, cutting it cleanly in two (the snap, the puff of acrid smoke). How he had carried the lawn mower to the basement to replace the cord, and what he said when he mowed over the new cord the very next week. All the while, I was thinking, Kathy, you idiot, this man is dying, and the last words he is going to hear are, "You smelled of grass and burning insulation." But eventually he fell asleep, jerking a little, and several days later, my father died. Now he knows if being dead is what he thought it would be—lilacs and apple blossoms, and his alarm clock gone.

And only a few years later, I was humming along with my heart's jagged song, my daughter was turning the corner on her sock, and her boyfriend was reading in the corner as Troy fell. Before the afternoon was over, the hospital released me to the custody of my daughter, as if I were a juvenile delinquent. There's no rule that says your heart has to beat a steady rhythm, I told the doctors. Think syncopation. Think jazz. But they gave me pills to steady this improvisational heart and let me go to my daughter's apartment. Safe in her kitchen, I tried to fix her a cup of tea, and she tried to fix me a cup of tea, and in the confusion we laughed a lot and cried maybe just a little.

THERE MAY HAVE BEEN a time when it made sense to think the earth was a parent who gave us life, fed us, cooled us, cleaned us, rocked us, instructed us, sang to us. But the metaphor is getting more complicated in a hurry. How many insults can a body endure before its natural healing processes give out and it starts to change? The land and the seas will endure, but the great systems that sustain us—Earth's life-giving cycles, the circles of heating and cooling, plants breathing in and breathing out, the cycles of the seasons, the great ocean currents—are changing in ways we don't understand. What are we to do, we lonely children, telling stories in the night?

There's no way around this: we must become the caretakers of our places. We have to take moral responsibility for the well-being of the air, the water, the land. And if this makes our relation to the earth complicated and painful, maybe that shouldn't come as a surprise. "A change is required of us," Linda Hogan wrote in *Dwellings*. "Caretaking is the utmost spiritual and physical responsibility of our time, and perhaps that stewardship is finally our place in the web of life, our work, the solution to the mystery of who we are."

But say you accept that. Say you agree that humans have an obligation to care for the earth. What does that mean in particular, in this place and time? What are you going to do? The point I want to make is that it isn't easy to know. You can't assume you know what to do. Everything changes around you, and you can't do nothing, but something is often the wrong thing. And what you do in one place has unexpected effects a hundred miles away or a hundred years in the future.

I had brought salmon as a gift to my father, alder-smoked salmon, the finest gift from the place I live. But his kidneys were too damaged to handle the salt, and just the smell of it made him sick. I should have known that. "Please," he begged, "get rid of it." So I dropped the salmon into a paper bag, stepped out the back door of his house, and walked to the trash can under a dark sky, where ozone fingered thin air, and great currents of wind warmed in unpredictable ways. Near my home on the other side of the continent, the Willamette River moved swiftly through the rock-lined channel that engineers built to guide the river on a straight course, undermining the ash-tree swales and carrying away the islands. In the great Columbia, salmon nosed against the dams that blocked their routes upstream. And in my father's yard, a single killdeer called and called from the dark beyond the fence. What is to be done?

MY STUDENT SAYS that where she lives, a person might say, "Do you kin that?" and mean, do you understand? She thinks that *kin* may be a local pronunciation of *ken*, which means to know or to see, but she's not sure. She thinks there must be a kind of knowledge that is like kinship, the understanding that comes with growing up in a family, staying close, living together for a very long time—a way of knowing that is all mixed up with loving and getting along. *Kenship,* a way of knowing, that comes from *kinship,* a way of being related. If there is this kind of knowledge, this is what we need, now, to respond to the ecological crises that have become part of the human condition.

This may be what Aldo Leopold meant when he said that the good work of caring for the land requires humble science, a humility that has its roots, like the word *humus*, in the very soil. It has to do with ecological literacy, a basic understanding of how the world works. It has to do with a kind of openness of eyes and ears, yes, but also of heart and mind. It has to do with compassion, literally, *suffering with*—the moral imagination that allows one to feel what another feels. It has to do with awe-filled observation, and growing up together. The difficult art of love.

Care has many meanings; one isn't enough. *To care for* means to have a love or fondness for. *To care for* means to attend to the needs of. But before there were these verbs, there was the noun, the root of all caring. *Care* comes from the Greek word *karas*, a lament, a song of sadness.

I hold all this in my mind as I try to grasp what it means to say that humankind must be the caretakers of the earth. What, then, is to be done? This is not a professor's test question; I have no idea of the answer, and just phrasing the question scares me. The impulse is to improvise wildly, to do whatever we need to do to get by another day. But how long can that go on?

We never do enough for our parents, and our timing is off at critical times. But isn't sitting with them part of the caring we must do?—to be in touch with our place in the family, to be attentive to the pain and mortality that are part of being alive, to tell stories about who we are in relation to the people and places we love, and sometimes, to sit quietly in the dark and cry.

THE MORAL EQUIVALENT
OF WILDNESS

I BACK-PADDLED IN my kayak, listening for small sloshes and hushed voices, the sounds of young people launching boats in the dark. Boat by boat, they disappeared across the lake—two kayaks, a canoe, a raft, a dory. The night was intensely quiet and dark, the way a campsite is quiet and dark after the fire goes cold. But the silhouette of the mountains was appearing against the sky in the east, and light seemed to be gathering in a particular cleft of the mountains. The lake showed a slick of silver.

I began to see the boats on the lake—scattered shadows, simply floating. One after another, the boats turned toward the light, stirring silver rings in dark water, until each boat pointed to the place in the mountains where the moon would emerge. In time, it did; just the top of its arc bulging through a space between black peaks, swelling upward, until the whole creamy white moon popped away from the mountains and floated free. When I looked behind me, the lake was dotted with uplifted, moonlit faces.

They were still for a very long time, the young people in the little drifting boats. Then I heard oars splash and the dory moved slowly up the bright pathway toward the moon, until the boat disappeared into the mountains' moon-shadow. Then the boat pivoted, and back they came again into the moonlight. They rested a moment in the glow of the moon, then back they went into moon-shadow. Pacing with the slowness of a heavy boat, they rowed back and forth, into the light, into the shadow. At first I couldn't understand what they were doing, but then it dawned on me that each time they went into the darkness, they made the moon drop back behind the mountains. And when they returned to the light, the moon rose: setting and rising, setting and rising, this great enlightenment, over and over again.

As the moon sailed higher in the sky and the night grew colder, the boats came in one by one, oars thumping damply, voices whispering goodnight. I counted them as they came. Allen will spend the night in a canoe, floating on that skim of moonlight. Jenna will spread a sleeping bag in the meadow; I saw the beam of her flashlight wander through the pines. When I walked back to my tent, I passed Alicia wrapped in a blanket, ankle deep in shallow water, watching the stars. My god, that must be cold; by morning, there would be frost. It was a long time before the dory came to shore. I lay in my tent and listened to voices murmur on the lake. "So what *is* nature?" one voice asked, making me smile. "And *where* is it?" another one answered.

IN THE MORNING, we all sat in sunlight that made us squint, reading Henry David Thoreau. This was PHL 438, Philosophy of Nature. Every year in late September, I take a group of university students to the mountains for this class. The students come from all parts of campus—marine biology, political science, geography, forestry, a few from philosophy. We camp on a little lake in a sub-alpine-fir and white-pine forest, just under the broken talus slopes of Jigsaw Mountain. In the meadow where we'd convened, frost glittered on each seed head and blade of grass, and steam rose in scarves from the lake.

A person "needs wildness the way a garden needs its load of muck," Thoreau wrote, and none of us disagreed, there in the meadow with light in our hair and dragon-flies clattering past and a great cloud of mayflies rising into sunlight for one ecstatic day of flight. We tried to imagine what the metaphor might mean exactly. What is muck? What is muck to a garden? How and when is it best applied? If plants need muck in heaps at their roots, where they live and grow, what is the significance of this horticultural fact for young people who for five days had been gorging on wildness, swallowing it in great gulps, as if they were starved.

Thoreau went on. "In wildness is the preservation

of the world." But the students noticed he didn't waste much time talking about wildness itself. He talked instead about what the muck of wildness nourishes in *people*—energy, strength, courage, independence, a new alertness, a way of seeing that penetrates ordinary expectations, joyous gratitude that goes beyond mere gratefulness to a state of grace. If the world is to be preserved, he implied, it will be because of the transformation wildness makes in people, their strength and joy and moral resolve.

The students thought they knew pretty much what Thoreau meant, because each of them had been transformed that week into the sort of person who canoes on a wilderness lake in the dark, in the silence, in the presence of the moon, in the grace and protection of their friends. They knew that swelling up inside. They knew that gratitude. They knew that connection to the lifting, moonlit night, the joy that can't be distinguished from love.

So here is what really scared me: The next day, the students would come down from the mountain to the first day of classes on a state university campus going through rush. The cars they'd left in empty parking lots would be shoulder to shoulder with pickups and bikes, and the cafeteria cashiers would be harried and cross. Voice mails would spill out invitations, and parties would thump long into the night. Between beers, the students would worry about how to find space in the classes they need, and how to open a checking account with no money. And when they called home to say they were safely out of the woods—yes, it was awesome, yes, yes—what would they be able to tell their parents, as the cell phone kicked in and out and somebody's car alarm beeped and the line for registration pushed out the door?

Can we bring the values of wild places with us as we drive down the mountain? How can we hold on to them in our neighborhoods? This was not an idle question. What if it's true that we need wildness the way a garden needs muck, that the "preservation of the world" depends on wildness? What if it's also true that most people don't live in the wild anymore, that we can't? What, then, will nourish and preserve us?

In the nearby places, is it possible to find the "moral equivalent of wildness," the way William James searched for the "moral equivalent of war"? James noticed that war, for all its hideous purpose and effect, sometimes brings out human characteristics that we value: It can make people brave and selfless and bring them together into communities of purpose. Wildness also changes human beings in ways we value: We come from the wild places restored, we say, which must have something to do with new stores that will nourish us, new sources of strength and peace, or maybe with new stories of who we are in relation to each other and the moon. If so, then without deep lakes and mountaintops in our daily lives, what we need in the cities is the moral equivalent of wildness. But what would that be?

The students wandered off in small groups, carrying notebooks and steaming cups of tea, down the trail past green moss heaped in a black-bottomed spring. I like to watch students talk among themselves, their heads bent together. Between their leaning bodies, light glittered on the lake. But the students no sooner left than I started wondering about the question they'd taken with them.

I'd been presupposing that wildness is something we find in the mountains and don't find in the valley, something we might transport from nature into culture, from wilderness to town, from far to near. But maybe this is wrong. Isn't there night in the city? Isn't there darkness? Doesn't the moon rise over the sororities when it rises also over the howling hills? Doesn't moisture lift from the broad lawns and catch on the eaves of the library, and doesn't that dampness smell of rivers and the sea? And when the students are sleeping in who knows what combinations in whatever pizza-box-strewn apartments, isn't the moon still there, sailing in the dark?

Maybe wildness isn't something we need to bring down from the mountain. It's true that legally designated Wilderness Areas are "out there," distant from our daily lives. Cartographers can draw lines around Wilderness. But there are no boundaries to wildness. In the warm afternoon, carbon dioxide from the cities creeps up the valleys and lifts into the clouds. In the cool night, air drifts down again, the smell of pines fingering between the Chevron and the 7-Eleven, glistening in the street-lights, whispering through the valves of our hearts. We are wildness—soil, water, oxygen, sunlight. It's all there is.

Maybe I should have asked the question differently: Maybe not how can we *bring* wildness into our lives, but how can we *remember to notice* the wildness in every sweating pore, each stewed carrot, every solid step, the morning air noisy with rain, the reeling stars? Or maybe this is the question: How can we live *as if we were* in the wilderness, with that same respect and care for what is beautiful and beyond us?

AFTER DINNER, THE CAMPFIRE pulled us in. A group campground at night is a beautiful thing, the little flashlights moving randomly around the dark space like fireflies as people gather up their books and pull an extra sweater from their tents. In the firelight, a pair of hands flicked chords from a guitar. A beam of light flashed over the boats pulled up on the beach.

As it turned out, I didn't teach the first lesson that night—how to wave out the flame in a marshmallow without slinging it across the fire into someone else's chest. Actually, I was doing very little of the teaching. One afternoon, the engineering major taught us why waves curl around a rock. The geography major tried to teach the botany major how to read trail maps. The forestry student helped us recognize firs—"Silver stripes under the leaves, like a Ferrari, fir, get it?" she said. For reasons I still don't understand, the philosophy major wanted to teach everyone the words to a song that started, "Her name was Lola." It's important, I think, that students do the teaching—not just exchanging facts, although that's important—but finding creative ways to help us all understand with our hearts and minds.

This is what the students had been thinking about that afternoon.

So what do we value in the experience of the wild and far away? What is this nourishing muck Thoreau talks about? Can we find an equivalent in our nearby lives?

"Some of it is silence," said Stephen, a tall environmental science major who had roofed his tent with garbage bags. "Wildness is a kind of silence, and silence is wild. You can bring silence down from the mountain, or you can find it in yourself—either way. The importance of silence is that it allows you to hear." As I understood him, the wildness value that Stephen and his study group were looking for was a kind of awareness, an intensity of listening, a way of sensing—really feeling—your connection to the great out-there. Stephen leaned toward the fire.

"We're going back into a noisy place and it isn't going to be easy to find silence, so we should practice," he said. "So our group decided to ask you not to speak for a half hour. Starting now. You'll know when the time is up."

The students were startled; silence is not their forte. But they were game. Some wandered out of the circle of light and made their way to the edge of the water. Three of them linked arms and leaned their heads on each others' shoulders. I sat at the base of a pine in the dark and watched fire play on the students' faces. Pushing through the pines, a breeze reached into the fire pit and lifted a spray of sparks into the stars. Then there was no sound but the snap of the fire and the ringing of the brilliant, brittle, black night.

At first, I wanted the time to pass quickly: we had

material to cover. Then I wanted it to last forever: maybe this silence was our most important material. Finally, from the lake came a lamentation, like the sound the mountains might make if they found a way to express the meaning of a million years. This would be Thom, who packed bagpipes among his essentials. I pictured him kneeling in a canoe, marking the end of the silence. Students reassembled by the fire, still silent. "Time's up," Stephen said. "You can talk now." But for the longest time, nobody did.

"This is a story my father gave me. His grandfather gave it to him. I am giving it to you." Carrie spoke from the darkness beyond the fire's circle of light. "A long time ago, the people were asleep in their village when they heard a great crashing in the forest. The warriors leapt to their feet and children hid in their robes. Everyone was frightened by the sound of a strong wind, the cracking of branches, thunderous thumping. In the morning, the men of the village went out to see what had happened. They found a long trail of broken branches and upended soil. All the cottonwoods had left the forest and marched to the edge of the river. That's where the men found the trees in the morning. And no one knows why."

The students stirred in their lawn chairs. The fire popped and a stream of sparks rose past the pines.

"So," Carrie said, "what's the most important part of this story?"

I didn't know. No one knew. I was afraid to guess.

One student began to explain the relation of water to plants of the riparian edge, but his words soon trailed off.

"The most important part is the last sentence; that no one knows why the trees went to the river. It's a mystery." Carrie paused.

"Is mystery a good thing, or a bad thing?"

Silence still.

"I believe mystery is a good thing. The great mystery isn't an enemy to fight or a hole to fill. It's a source of strength and comfort. The existence of so much that we don't understand is a gift to us. That great mystery is what wildness is, and wildness is a great mystery."

More silence, but now it was getting edgy. The wind chilled my back and I pulled my hood over my head. The circle moved a little closer to the fire. Then Franz threw another alder log on the fire, and in a shower of sparks, people moved their chairs back a step.

"It's fine to talk about silence and mystery, so yeah, okay." This was Katherine. "But the fact is that what we value up here in the wild is finally to be in a place that is beautiful and healthy and not all screwed up—those views across a lake that isn't polluted to a mountain that isn't clear-cut, and stars we can actually see, and birds that aren't full of tumors, and a river not crammed with old tires and shopping carts and silt. So, okay, in one sense, wildness is everywhere, even in the city. But that's not what people mean when they talk about wildness; they mean a place that isn't trampled half to death. And it's not just about beauty. You destroy a place and you destroy your own place, and your health, and your hopes."

Sorrow in students terrifies me. I never know what to do. "What does this tell us," I asked, "about our responsibilities?" I knew I was floundering, but you can't lead students to a bitter place and leave them there. "If Katherine is right, and what we value about the experience of the wild is the chance to live for a time in a healthy, clean, bird-filled place, then what do we have to do when we come down from the mountain?" The question hung for a long time in the firelight.

But this was okay with me: if there's a question, at least there's the chance for an answer. Maybe moral resolve is the highest value of wildness, the wild flash of awareness that the ecological wholeness of the natural world requires a moral integrity as well.

When we drove down the mountains the next day, we would drive past a set of dams that control the Willamette River as it flows past their hometown. They know the effect on the river of dams a hundred miles away: we began this class on the barren river island that had once grown a forest—before the dams held back the sediment that would have replenished the soil. They understand the connection between near and far away.

Between the wilderness and the town, we would drive through a series of ecological and political landscapes— from the primeval forests, through clear-cuts and tree farms as patchy and tufted as if a child had taken electric clippers to the back of a dog, on through the laser-leveled agricultural fields, to the neighborhoods. On the same journey, we would pass through a set of equally distinct moral landscapes. We would begin in patches of wilderness ethic, where people feel a strong obligation to do no harm, and where hikers enter the land with respect and rejoicing. At the end of the journey are hedge-bordered home places, where people care for the land as if it were a child, tending to its needs, making it beautiful and healthy. But in between is a wide, bewildering swath of moral no-man's-land, where the land is a commodity and people are careless of it, or disdainful, and use it for their own short-term self-interest.

But if we want to take wildland values down from the mountain, don't we also take home our moral obligation to care for what we value in land wherever we find it—silence and mystery, beauty, the health of systems that sustain life? In a world so ecologically connected, what sense does it make to live by different moral codes in different places?

The discussion went on for a long time that night— the soft voices, the rising sparks, the stars tangled in the pines like Christmas lights, and then a prolonged and thoughtful silence. Finally Marissa, a philosophy major from Georgia, stood up, and so did we all, in a circle around the fire. "I want everybody to hum a note and hold it," she said. "Doesn't matter what note. Just start to hum and don't stop."

And so we did, young people and their professor, standing close to the fire, bundled in the oddest assortment of coats and mittens, wearing hats we haven't taken off for a week. Everybody hummed their own note, and it was a crazy, discordant chord we made.

But gradually—inevitably—the voices tuned themselves together into a rich, beautiful, lingering chord. In the wild night, in the firelight, the students' eyes were bright with tears.

🐝

AS THE SUN ROSE the next morning, I heard thin sheets of ice slide off my tent and tinkle against the ground. The pump handle squeaked rhythmically as someone filled the pails for coffee—almost always Ina, up early. Two people, surely Todd and Josh, tiptoed past my tent and walked out on a log that reached over the water. I heard a splash, then another, the sucked-in-breath and muffled cries, then the slog toward shore. Running shoes crunched on the path as Shawna headed out on her daily search for a bear. The outhouse door thumped. Steller's jays called in the snowberries. A tent zipped open. It was the morning of the last day.

🐝

Study Questions

1. *Demonstrate how to:*
   (a) get into a kayak without getting your sneakers wet,
   (b) predict the phase of the moon,
   (c) find north,
   (d) define nature, and,
   (e) distinguish a vulture from a bald eagle in flight.

2. *What happens when you poke one of those blisters on a Douglas-fir trunk? Therefore, what? How many ways does a dragonfly see the world? Therefore, what? Where do the stars go during the day? Therefore, what? How deep is the lake? Therefore, what? What matters most to you? Therefore, what?*

3. *Compare and contrast:*
   (a) The call of a great horned owl, an approaching storm.
   (b) Todd's hat, a pumpkin.
   (c) Dusk, dawn.
   (d) A dragonfly larva, a dragonfly adult.
   (e) You in the mountains, you in town.

4. *List twelve changes you could make in your own life to nurture healthy communities of renewal in the places where you live. Multiply 12 by 6,369,866,054 people. (If you answer this question at the end of the term, multiply by 6,375,882,069.)*

5. *"Anything you can do or dream you can, begin it. Boldness has genius, power, and magic in it." (Goethe). Explain. Use examples.*

THE PARABLES OF THE
RATS AND MICE

I.

"A MOUSE WAS CRUSHED," Jon said as he loaded
the tent bag into the boat. He and Frank and I had been
camping on a gravel bar in the Willamette River, not far
from home.

I looked up from my oatmeal.

"What are you talking about?"

"A mouse died under our tent."

"Of what?"

"Crushing."

Nobody talks this way.

"What kind of mouse?" I asked. "How crushed?"

"Deer mouse, I guess," Jon said. "Very."

I'm not the kind of person who won't kill if I need to.
Slapping flies. Boiling crabs alive. Bashing a fresh-caught

trout on the head. These things don't bother me all that much. But an innocent mouse ruptured like a water balloon under my hips while I roll around dreaming that we had adopted a baby girl named Guernica—this grieves me. I have no doubt I'm the one who squashed it. I'm dreaming of having too many committee obligations to take care of little Guernica. A mouse cowers under my hips. Then one more missed committee meeting and I roll this mouse flat as a cartoon.

"It was under my sleeping pad, wasn't it," I demanded.

Jon wouldn't answer. But Frank said it all by changing the subject. "Why did you name the baby Guernica?" he asked.

"I didn't name her. She came that way. But I was too busy to take care of her, so I was trying to think of a way to give her back," I said.

So many things you can't explain.

"Actually," Jon said, "it was pretty bloody."

I can understand how a gravity-drenched being can steamroller a mouse. What I have a harder time understanding is how human beings of good will can do so much harm. Not, how is it possible to do harm?—human beings have made a science of that. But, how do we live with ourselves, go merrily on our little ways, knowing that we are destroying things we cherish?

A mouse was crushed, we say. The forest was cut. The birds were poisoned. An opossum was run over. A good time was had by all. So nobody's acting here, only being acted upon. A human being walks by and mice keel over, trees sever themselves cleanly at the knees and plop into the dirt, birds plummet from the sky, and opossums pop into the air, dissolve into fluids, and distribute themselves randomly over the asphalt. The passive voice, the sentence where the causal agent has gone missing. The facts are bad enough, but the grammar is terrifying.

Species go extinct, we say. But the fact of the matter is that species don't always go extinct, the way bananas go bad, or bombs go astray, or elderly uncles go crazy or go about their business. Human decisions sometimes drive animals to extinction. Human decisions extinguish entire species. Extinguish: to cause to cease burning. All the little sparking lives.

Shit happens, we say. And sometimes it does. But the fact of the matter is that sometimes, shit doesn't just happen. Sometimes, human beings deliberately create the conditions under which shit is more likely to occur.

Nobody says it's easy, knowing the difference between right and wrong. Is it what you *intend* that makes all the difference, or what actually *happens* as a result of what you do, no matter what you intend? Everybody makes mistakes, nobody can see into the future, and isn't too great an eagerness to lay blame a moral failing too? I think about this story and wonder what it means. One thing, I think, is clear: I should go on full alert if I hear myself say, "I'm not the one who does harm; harm just happens around me." Like it or not, I own the consequences of my acts. They're mine. That mouse is mine.

II.

IN A MOUNTAIN CABIN in Colorado many years ago, when Frank and I were very young, we were annoyed each night by a pack rat. It was a lovely brown rat with a softly furred tail, but it pooped on the dish towels and skittered and crashed all night long, chewing up tin foil and Styrofoam cups. Plus, it was a prime suspect in the disappearance of a bike-lock key. Not really capital offenses, as I think about it now, but we decided to put out poison. In those days, rat poison was a waxy substance in bottle caps. Fools, we put out two. In the morning, one of the bottle caps was gone, and in its place, the rat had left a quarter.

Western philosophy has made a whole moral theory out of trade-offs like this. "An act is right if it creates the greatest happiness for the greatest number," we assure each other: the famous Utilitarian Principle. So anything can be traded, as long as you're a sharp trader, always getting a balance of happiness over the long run. Dam the Columbia River, for example. Ruin ancient runs of lamprey and sockeye salmon, bury the places where native people have gathered for centuries to fish and to pray, as long as you can show on a graph how the benefits soar beyond the measured costs, irrigating orchards and sending cheap electricity to California. We do the calculation—this much pleasure, that much pain—and if the balance of happiness is in the black, we assure ourselves that we are acting morally.

Well, maybe we are and maybe we aren't. It's complicated.

Aren't there some things that can't be traded, not even for happiness? Some things are irreplaceable: too wonderful, too precious, too fundamental to be traded for anything. This is no secret. What parent would knowingly trade away her child's health? And what about other things we value for their own sake, not for what they can give us? The wild Sierras, and the wildflowers that flatten against the rocks in thunderstorms. The night sky. The turning of the seasons. An old man.

And even if everything could be traded, why is happiness always the most valuable of all the chits? The "greatest good" theory is built on the arrogant and dubious idea that human beings are the center of the universe and human happiness is the purpose of all creation. Human beings, imagining that the world and everything in it—the forests, the lakes, the great flocks of cranes—were made especially for them, the way ticks must think that hikers are their special gifts from God. Our temptation is to design arrogant policies and make dubious decisions, and then we end up doing to the natural world what ticks do to us, except that ticks have the good grace to drop off when their stomachs are full. I don't know: It's too convenient, that ethical theory should suddenly affirm the human race's single-minded search for happiness and forget about everything else we and the rest of creation might need and seek.

In the end, I don't think you can trade rights and wrongs on the open market. I don't think it will do to say, I don't actually do anything wrong in this place and time, as long as my act brings about happiness somewhere else.

III.

MY FATHER WAS A BOY during the Depression, in a family with never enough money to go around. He saw economic opportunity in a matchbox advertisement for dancing mice. Dancing mice are little house mice with a genetic abnormality that interferes with their ability to balance. So dancing mice stagger and spin in a drunken tarantella—an entertainment, maybe, in a grim time.

My father saved up his paper-route money and sent away for a pair. The way mice breed, he was sure he'd have a dozen mice every few months and could sell them door-to-door. Surely everyone wants a dancing mouse. After a while, two mice came in the mail, as promised. But they didn't seem to like each other, and within a week, one died. Hoping at least to recoup his initial investment, my father went from house to house in his neighborhood, giving mouse-dancing demonstrations, until he found a buyer—an elderly woman who lived alone. She gave him a quarter and took the mouse.

"What happened then?" I asked my father.

"I don't know," he said.

One of the factors that makes moral reasoning difficult is that so many of the consequences of our acts are invisible. What we care about the most is often the hardest to locate and measure. How does beauty enter into a calculus? How does forgiveness, or the grace in a rainwashed morning, or the dignity of undisturbed land? What is the measurable value of a neighborhood? What unit of measurement do you use? Jeremy Bentham, the father of Utilitarianism, suggested a "Utile," but that never quite caught on. The industrialized economy has substituted the U.S. dollar. But if you have to put a dollar value on everything, then before you know it, the dollar is the only thing that has value. You make your charts, graphing out the benefits and the costs, but the very fact of measuring and charting tips the scales toward what can be measured and charted, or what can be traded for cash.

The moral of the story? I think it's this: It won't work to say, I don't do harm if what I destroy has no dollar value, or if I have no way to measure what happens as a result of my decisions. These are evasions, or denials.

IV.

THIS ONE IS JON'S STORY. I wasn't there, but I'll try to do it justice. In the wilderness Alaska research camp where Jon works summers, a baby pine marten turned up tangled in a fishnet in a storage shed. A pine marten is a large silky weasel, not a rodent, but close enough for this essay, I hope. And it's fierce—the hiss, the flashing teeth, the predator's slashing speed. Hearing the baby squeal, the two young aquatic biologists struggled to untangle it. They're used to releasing fish, but a panicked mammal was a different challenge. Add to the mix the frantic mother marten, crouching with her teeth bared and launching toward their ankles.

I can imagine the shouting and dodging, the strategic retreats and contingency plans, the clever use of long-handled tools, the quick reflexes and equally quick laughter, the relief and beers all around when the marten finally flashed from their hands and disappeared. What seems important to me about this story is that neither of the men wondered whether they should release the baby marten, whether they should risk the nasty bites to set it free. The only issue was how.

Philosophers say that you can't deduce an *ought* from an *is*. It's the old "is-ought problem" that has bedeviled Western philosophy since the eighteenth century, when David Hume explained that from a mere description—this is the way the world is—you can't infer a prescription—this is the way the world ought to be. In one sense, he's right: You can stare at the world as long as you want, examine it every which way in all its detail, and it will not reveal to you what ought to be. But that doesn't mean you can't infer what you ought to do, from a description of the way the world is. We do it all the time. Jon made that leap in a flash, the space of a synapse, so fast he was probably never aware of the jump: The marten is caught in the net; therefore, I ought to free it.

Logically speaking, the bridge linking "what is" and "what ought to be" is a hidden premise: If a marten is caught in my net, then I ought to free it. The premise is a description, not about the world, but about the moral convictions of the person acting in the world. To reason from facts to moral duties, a person has to take a stand: "Under these circumstances, this is what I ought to do." In taking this stand, in supplying the link between physical and moral worlds, he creates himself as a moral agent and defines his character.

Who is the person who would look at a squealing animal, rock back on his heels, say, "There is no moral obligation in this scene," and walk away? There may be no moral obligation in the scene, but there is a moral obligation in the presence of a person in the scene, a particular person stopped in his tracks by that set of facts, a particular person who embodies a set of unspoken principles about who he is and how he ought to act in the world. The quick judgment, the moral impulse, the silent premise affirming one's standing as a moral agent, the sharp knife against the tough strands of a net: this may be humanity's unique gift to the universe.

V.

LAST TERM, VIOLA CORDOVA came to my class to talk about taking moral responsibility. She was a wonderful person and a friend, a laughing, chain-smoking Jicarilla Apache woman with a philosophy doctorate from the University of New Mexico. Everything is connected, she told my students, and on the chalkboard she drew a stone dropping into a lake. The ripples spread out and out in widening circles and rocked the cattails by the shore. She paused to draw cattails, an arrow showing how they gently rocked. The students understood that every decision they make, every action they undertake, has spreading consequences in the real world, the world of water and sky and striving. And so they have to take responsibility, acknowledging that everything they do or fail to do creates the world in the next moment. They are co-creators of the universe, bringing into being the world where they will live.

A blood vessel burst in Viola's brain the week after her lecture, killing her and shaking my students to the core. They turned back through their notes to find the ideas she had given them, all finding the drawings they had copied off the board. Ripples reaching out toward shore.

So one more story, this one with a happy ending. Our daughter Erin and her friend Jenny launched a canoe onto a lake in Wisconsin, after brushing out the pine needles that had accumulated over the summer. When they were well out on the water, a deer mouse squeezed from the bulkhead and started running up and down the length of the canoe.

"Before we could react, which means before we could climb onto the seats and dump the canoe," Erin said, "the mouse jumped into the drink. But it didn't know the direction to shore and it swam in tighter and tighter circles. So Jenny threw it one of those orange life jackets, and when she nudged the mouse in that direction with her paddle, the mouse climbed onto the collar."

Jenny pushed along the life jacket with its little pas-
senger, Erin paddled the canoe, and the three of them
zigzagged toward land. When they were close to safety,
with the canoe between the life jacket and the shore, the
mouse leapt onto the canoe, ran across a thwart, jumped
into the water on the far side, and swam to the bank.
What I like to think about, to picture in my mind, is a
mouse dog-paddling between the cattails, pushing a tiny
bow wave toward shore.

I can't say I always, or even often, know what is right.
But I'm pretty well convinced that whatever I do—what
I decide to do and what I do without deciding—shapes
the world and shapes me as a moral agent. Perhaps
humans are the only beings in the universe capable of
regret and resolve. If this is so, then the most important
question is how—by what sort of education or process of
moral development—does a person come to grow these
moral synapses, this strong sense that the world-as-it-is
asks something of them.

THE WORLD DEPENDS
ON THIS

THE MESSAGE MACHINE WAS blinking when I got home from work: "First, I want you to know that your daughter is going to be fine." I braced myself for whatever would come next. "She was arrested during the antiwar demonstrations. They're holding her in the San Francisco County Jail."

Frank and I had been watching world news all day. Now suddenly, this wasn't about world news. It was about our daughter and a parent's fears. What will she eat? How can she sleep? Do the handcuffs cut her wrists?

The night before, I had dreamed about Erin. She was one of the young people in an outdoor clothing catalog, striding out in autumn colors, her hair as bright as apricots. Wearing a skirt the color of pumpkins, she'd leaned against the other young people, laughing. But she wasn't in some dreamy, sun-saturated place now; she was sitting in a small cube of light in a darkened jail.

I tried to picture a jail at night. Do the other inmates sleep splay-legged and heavy on their backs? Do they curl up as if they were babies? And our daughter?—surely she's sitting awake on a bench with her knees to her chest and her arms wrapped around them. She'd be cold, in that dark place.

Babies startle if they aren't wrapped tightly. We learned this in a child-care class before she was born. Their bodies twitch and their arms flail as they sleep, and if nothing is holding them, they are afraid. So you have to wrap a newborn baby. We held our daughter close and wrapped her in blankets, tight as corn in the husk.

We loved her so much and raised her so carefully, and isn't this what all parents do if they can? Piano lessons, art lessons, a hundred-dollar safety seat for the car. When she learned to drive, we tried to keep track of where she went and when she would be home. It never occurred to us that she would go to jail.

So here is the first thing she said when she called collect from the holding cell: "What can I say to keep you from worrying?"

To keep a parent from worrying?

Tell us you're home in bed, I cried, but Frank took the phone from my hand. She told him she was in a holding cell with dozens of other women. They are strong, amazing women, many of them mothers and grandmothers, many elegantly dressed in black, she said, and Frank thought that Erin's own voice was strong and amazing, more certain than he'd ever heard it.

To pass the time, the women are teaching each other to dance, she said. They're placing calls to news agencies, but they can't get through. Bombs are falling, newspapers aren't answering their phones, injustice and environmental destruction tangle in nets of violence and profit around the world—and all these beautiful women are in jail.

The police released Erin at 2:30 A.M. A friend came into the city to drive her home.

Don't all parents want the world for their children? *Fellow parents, tell me, wouldn't we do anything for them?* To give them big houses, we will cut ancient forests. To give them perfect fruit, we will poison their food with pesticides. To give them the latest technologies, we will reduce entire valleys to toxic dumps. To give them the best education, we will invest in companies that profit from death. To keep them safe, we will deny them the right to privacy, to travel unimpeded, to peacefully assemble. And to give them peace, we will kill other peoples' children or send them to be killed, and amass enough weapons to kill the children again, kill them twenty times if necessary.

We would do anything for our children but the one big thing: Stop and ask ourselves, what are we doing and allowing to be done? I looked again at the shopping list Frank had scribbled on as he talked to Erin: *Toilet paper / Bourbon / Flowers / County Jail / War protest / Inmate / Dave 415-516-6372.* How everyday and ordinary are our disastrous decisions. Frank and I go busily about, buying this or that, voting or not, burning up gasoline or jet fuel or split pine—on a small scale, in the short term, making things work for our children—forgetting that whatever is left of the world is the place where they will have to live.

What will our grandchildren say? I think I can guess:

How could you not have known? What more evidence did you need that your lives, your comfortable lives, would do so much damage to ours?

Did you think you could wage war against nations without waging war against people and against the earth? Didn't you wonder what we would drink, once you had poisoned the aquifers? Didn't you wonder what we would breathe, once you poisoned the air? Did you stop to ask how we would be safe, in a world poisoned by war?

Did you think it all belonged to you—this beautiful earth?

You, who loved your children, did you think we could live without clean air and healthy cities? You, who loved the earth, did you think we could live without birdsong and swaying trees?

And if you knew, how could you not care? What could matter more to you than your children, and their babies? How could a parent destroy what is life-giving and astonishing in her child's world?

And if you knew, and if you cared, how could you not act? What excuses did you make?

And now, what would you have us do?

Two days after she got out of jail, we walked with Erin beside the ocean. Under a steep headland, we came across a jumbled heap of fishing nets, string, nylon cord and bullwhip kelp, intricately tangled. Buoys were smashed and buried beyond hope.

"This is what the world is," she said. She tugged at a rope in the nets gone to tangled ruin, drifted with sand.

"Yes. But you don't have to go to jail to say so. There are other ways," I said softly, knowing I should be still.

She answered as softly. "Then you need to show me those ways," she said. "Don't tell me. Show me."

Dear god. I don't know what to do: what to hope and what to fear, what to invest in and what to give up, what to insist on and what to refuse, how to go on with living in a time of death. All I know is how to hold my daughter, wrapping my arms tight around her shoulders. Right now, the world depends on this.

LEARNING TO DANCE

STEPPING OUT OF THE pickup into a cold wind, we
studied the map a friend had drawn on the back of an
envelope. It had no route numbers or identifying place
names, just lines and mileage figures—in case, our friend
had said, the map fell into the wrong hands. So. Another
mile on a gravel road, a right turn, another three miles
down a dirt track. Finally we came to a rusted metal sign
that stood in a bald patch of gravel between sagebrush.
STOP HERE, it said.

To get to this place, Frank and Jonathan and I
had driven all the way across the mountains from the
Willamette Valley to the Oregon high desert, five hard
hours on the road. The land that stretched away from
us was empty—not a juniper, not a telephone pole, not
a ranch house, not a fence line in any direction, nothing
but sagebrush, evenly spaced. There was a wash of snow
on mountains at the northern horizon, and what looked
like rain or sleet slanting from clouds in the south. The
only other element that gave any direction to the land

was the wind, blowing hard out of the west. Untethered by trees, the sky slowly rotated counterclockwise, a complicated pattern of rain clouds and wind lenses and sweeps of cirrus, and a band of yellow at the western horizon where the sun was about to set.

With an hour to wait, we pitched the tent on gravel between the sign and the pickup. I boiled water on the camp stove, handed a cup of tea to Jonathan, to Frank, then wrapped my hands around a cup of my own. Huddling in the lee of the truck, I was glad to have at least the illusion of a hill to my back—anything to break the sweep of the plains.

In dimming light, we pulled on warm clothes and walked a quarter mile down the dirt track past a dry stock pond, out into the sagebrush. There, we crouched behind a low log wall. Wind that had picked up dampness and winter over a hundred unbroken miles of upland lifted the edge of my windbreaker and saturated the air with noise. I settled deeper into my jacket, put binoculars to my eyes, and swept the area in front of me. Jonathan shifted his weight, jiggling his knees up and down like a marionette, trying to stay warm. Frank scanned the plains with heavy field glasses. As far as I could tell, there was nothing to see but sage and sand to the cupped edges of the earth.

Then, as if a conductor had lifted his baton, the wind fell silent. A single sage sparrow, then a madrigal chorus of sparrows, filled the air with thin threads of song. Over to the east, a horned lark sang *treeteeleetee treet.* The lights dimmed and suddenly a sage grouse appeared. He stood rigid and proud, with a chasuble of dazzling white draped around his neck. He stretched himself up to great heights, spread his neck feathers into a perfect blaze of white, and inflated two yellow sacs on his chest. The sacs expanded and then collapsed into the feathers, booming like timpani. Then, where there had been no bird, another grouse suddenly appeared, facing the first. His tail was a ruff of rigid spikes fanned flat against his rump, blazed with white spots.

The grouse puffed and strutted on their dancing ground, the *lek,* the place we had come so far to see. A lek is just a few square yards of desert—wind-twisted sagebrush, bare gravel, some dry wisps of grass, undistinguished. But for generations, this is the exact place the grouse have chosen to dance, coming a long way to dance on this particular ground.

From all quarters, dark forms sailed in on set wings. A dozen more grouse appeared out of nowhere, unfurling white ruffs and then folding them in under speckled feathers that had grown over generations to the exact color of the ground litter. They appeared and disappeared as if a spotlight were roving over the landscape, illuminating first one dancing bird and then another. Facing each other maybe four feet apart, they drew themselves up tall and splayed their feathers with such great effort that, even from fifty feet away, I could see them tremble.

I tried to follow all the birds as they danced around the lek, but they flashed and disappeared, only to reappear in another place, leaving me fussing with my binoculars. When I couldn't distinguish the birds from the bushes,

I gave up on binoculars and watched their silhouettes against the glow of dusk. Finally, the last of the birds vanished. We sat for a long time, exhilarated and silent, and maybe a little abashed, to have been uninvited observers of dancing so intimate and intense.

Back at the truck, we stood hunched to the wind and spooned stew into our mouths with our sleeves drawn over our hands. In the morning, we would hike back to the lek to inspect it in full light.

Abruptly, the wind shifted from west to north and snow moved in, big wind-driven pellets of snow. We piled the dirty dishes against the wheel of the truck so we could find them in the morning and crawled into the tent. Frank batted the side of the tent to dislodge the snow and we settled deep into our bags and went to sleep. During the night, I awoke to hear the softer, slipping sounds of dry snow, telling me the temperature was dropping and the wind had died.

WHEN MY SISTERS AND I were young, we danced in the basement. It was just a wood-paneled cellar, a place for the ironing board and furniture cast off from the living room, and a dehumidifier always churning away. My sisters and I grubbed around in the chest of drawers where we kept the dress-up clothes—every filmy or silky, gauzy or trailing, flowered or gold-threaded piece of clothing we could wheedle from our mother. We put these on over our clothes, cinching them around our waists with scarves, tying them behind us like trains. We put on lipstick, and then we chose our names.

My name was Mignonette, and we called our collective selves The Three Flowers. We put The Nutcracker Suite on the turntable and, as sugarplum fairy songs burbled into the basement air, we jumped off the furniture. This was dancing, to step up onto a chair and leap off, arms outspread, trailing rayon scarves. Then a quick spin, a curtsey, and we'd scramble to the back of the couch, jump from the back to the cushion, from the cushion to the floor, scarves flying. Over time, we incorporated new identities and new movements into our routine—a plié before the plunge, a pointed toe, a better name.

Some years later, after my mother decided we needed to learn social dancing, she convinced our school to hire a real teacher, Miss York, to come to the junior-high-school gym. So I grew up knowing how to fox-trot and cha-cha and waltz on a basketball floor, although the guys never could remember the steps, and what we called dancing in high school looked and felt a lot like what we called petting.

When I was a college student in Ohio, my friends and I danced on Friday nights at a place called the T.U.B., the temporary union building, just a garage fancied up with a Coke machine. We danced to Simon and Garfunkel—*I am a rock / I am an island*—and sang along, thinking maybe this was true.

But I never knew what dancing really was until Frank and I moved to a little tree-lined street filled with new families. I'm not sure how the tradition started,

but every year the neighbors got together to organize
a street dance. This was always a complicated endeavor
that involved the police, who blocked traffic, and miles of
extension cords. Everybody pulled out their Christmas
lights and strung them across the street. Then, when it
got dark and the colored bulbs came on and the little
band started to tune up, families came out of their houses
and danced under the trees in the street.

We did square dancing and reels—anything the band
thought they could teach people who mostly had PhDs
and couldn't tell left from right. "Red River Valley" and
something about blackbirds, a fiddle and guitar in the
band. With toddlers on our shoulders and babies bob-
bling up and down in packs, we do-si-doed and swung
our partners, lifting grandmothers and grade-school
kids off the ground. Two people would stretch on tiptoes
to make a bridge with their arms, and we would hold a
child's hand and duck through and come on around and
do it again. My face would be sore the next day from all
the smiling—I loved it that much.

And how can you not be neighbors with people
you've danced with, people part of a circle rotating in
the street, under the swinging, colored lights? That tree-
draped street became the center of a family of families
we called the Neighborhood. For years, we helped raise
each others' children and traded zucchinis for tall beers
on August nights.

But that was a long time ago, and one family eventually moved to a fancier part of town and people got
busy or successful, usually both; the family that was

the band moved to Portland for a better job; and there isn't dancing in that street anymore, and there isn't a Neighborhood.

So Frank and I are signed up for a ballroom dancing class this term. Frank dreads this, but he does it for me. The first class is tomorrow and I'm not optimistic. We have a long history of dropping out of dance classes as soon as we pay tuition. But I think it's important to try again. Surely, if we need to know anything, we need to know how to dance. Frank suggests that car repair or tax law might be more useful skills, but I don't listen.

I envy people who dance. My colleague Frank Lake returns to the Klamath River each year to join the Karuk people for the world renewal dances. The world creates the people, yes, as a mother creates her children, and brings the rain and salmon. And for better or worse, the people create the world, too. People burn grassfields to make the camas prairie and tend the huckleberry bushes. Or people overharvest the salmon and overgraze the land—this happens too. There is a reciprocal relationship between people and their places; people share with the world the responsibility for determining what the next year will bring. People and the world are co-creators of the future.

The families come together each year in their town, gathering from colleges and cities and ranch houses and fishing ports, to sing and dance, raising their voices, raising the dust, to do their part to create the new world. Dancing, Frank Lake says, is simultaneously an act of creation and an act of celebration of the ecological and moral relatedness of people and the places they live.

This seems right and good to me. And even though I don't live in a culture that dances the world renewal dances, and even though learning to dance has degenerated into a painful process involving teachers endlessly counting *ONE two three*, I'd like to think about how to celebrate the reciprocal relation I have to the places I live and acknowledge my role in what happens next. I'd like to find ways to create new communities of renewal.

✾

AT FIRST LIGHT, the high desert landscape sat gray and lumpy, covered with snow. The sky was lumpy and gray too, a mirror image of the land. We walked down the snowy ruts, crossed the tracks of a jackrabbit, and turned again toward the lek. I wanted to see this piece of land in full light, to feel it, to figure out what was different about it. What qualities of sand and gravel, what angle of light, what convergence of forces has made this the dancing place for so many generations of birds? My plan was to walk into the middle of the lek and lie on my back, look up to the piece of sky that covers this particular point, and hope to understand what it is that creates a chosen place.

I hesitated at the edge of the lek where the birds had danced in the dusk. Shadows grew around the sage—vague and gray, but a sign of dawn all the same. A sparrow sang. The breeze picked up. I began to understand that the birds had danced this lek into existence. The place made them, the speckled feathers and precise beaks; and they made the place. The lek was a scratchy, used-up patch, no wetter or drier, higher or lower, warmer or colder than a thousand other patches of sagebrush from here to the horizon. But this is where the birds come to dance. And by that dancing, they make it into a dancing ground. Humans should make a wide circle around these places and pass them by. There are places on this earth that are sacred because they are the places where sacraments take place.

The land shapes people and their communities, and the people shape the land. By their actions, they make it into a place of value and health, something to celebrate; or they degrade and debase it, making it something to avoid and despise. There *is* dancing on the land in the places I live, but it has become an ugly dance marathon to see who is left standing in the contest between people of development and people of conservation. The dance has been going on so long that the partners are exhausted. But they continue to dance, moving more and more slowly, leaning on each other to keep from falling, draping their arms over each others' shoulders, swaying, shuffling, staggering, moving to the music until they give up.

What I'd like to recover—or to invent—are new dances of celebration and reciprocity. We are of the towns and river valleys as much as the sage grouse are of the high desert plains. So let's learn how to celebrate this wheeling-and-spinning, do-si-do, all-partners-please-join-hands relation to the land. In the broad open spaces, in the gardens, in the wilderness, in the marketplaces, in the city parks and coffeehouses, in the neighborhoods, we can learn to dance. And then we can come together to dance the stars back into the sky, dance the neighborhoods back into the towns, dance the sacred back into our dusty patches of ground.

WHERE SHOULD I LIVE, AND WHAT SHOULD I LIVE FOR?

OUR LITTLE HOUSE SITS close by the university on a laurel-hedged lot that is fifty feet wide and a hundred feet long. Frank and I walk to work; the trip takes eight minutes. Day and night, I hear the pump on my neighbor's artificial waterfall, drowning out even the sound of rain on my own roof. The neighbor's bedroom window is ten feet from my own, and when she runs her clothes dryer, I breathe ClingFree fabric softener for hours. Sometimes I climb out the window to our rooftop porch, to sleep under the absence of stars in a pink glow that comes from the campus greenhouses—for some unimaginable, probably toxic, reason. When I look across the yard, I can count the pages as my neighbor reads under his spotted calfskin lamp.

I want to live in a house where I can watch coyotes out the window, a small glass and cedar house reflected in bright water that smells of juniper and melting snow.

A place so remote I can't see a light from any other house, and so near the stars that the constellations disappear in clouds of starlight. A place where pine siskins whisper me awake in the morning and chickadees land on my hand. During the working day, the place will sing in my ear and I will write down its words and wisdom, longhand. In the evenings, my family will come together to sit by a small fire, looking up with gentle smiles when our coyotes howl or migrating cranes fly overhead, bugling. I have dreamed all my life of living in this house.

I am a nature writer, by god. Nature writers ever since Thoreau have moved to the woods, deliberately, to learn what it has to teach. I know a writer who lives in a hemlock forest on the edge of Thimbleberry Bay, where humpback whales spout and the salt air is so thick it glistens in her hair. I know a nature writer who lives on a salmon stream in the Pacific coast range and looks out his window into the top of a Douglas-fir. Another lives on stilts over the tide. The outermost house. The long-legged house. A hut of one's own. The Shack. Listening Point. The trailer at the edge of Arches, the U.S. Forest Service fire lookout station. On a red canyon cliff, beside the Blackfoot River, on a Cape Cod marsh, on an island in Puget Sound, in Oregon's foggy coastal mountains.

Am I the only nature writer left in town? I'm ferociously jealous of writers who wake up to birdsong, and I'm nervous about the legup I imagine they must have, living so close to the sources of their inspiration. When I read their essays about living in place, I get depressed and anxious, worried that when I come to die, I will discover that I have not lived—just what Thoreau predicted. Or worse, I will write dully or stupidly of wild places, like a cave salamander describing a flight of crows.

Just go, I tell myself. Nothing in this world is stopping you. You have the money; you have the dream. Confess: you even have the floor plan. Find a beautiful place. Build your dream shack. Inhabit that place, just as the poets advise you to do. Learn the trees, record the arrival times of the geese, study the clouds, become that place and let it shape your thoughts and words.

But I don't go. Maybe I like my neighbors too much. Maybe I'm too cheap to commute to work. Honestly, realtors give me a rash. And maybe there's no place left for me anyway, so many people who love wild places have moved there. My Montana writer friend warns that someday soon one last nature lover will move to Montana and build one last log house on one last fifty-acre parcel, and the whole state will slowly tip and the lot of them will slide off into Lake Coeur d'Alene.

Ten years ago, Frank and I bought forty-five acres along the Marys River in Oregon. But it wasn't like you think; we didn't buy it because it was beautiful, although it was. We bought it like a person might shell out twenty bucks for a stray dog at the pound—falling instantly in love with something vulnerable and needing protection. So how can I build my Thoreauvian cabin there? We honestly don't know what to do with the land. So it just sits there; the creeks flood, the ash swales green up, the meadows fill with light and hawks and coyotes. Snakes multiply. And I live in town, twenty miles away, and pay the taxes, and think maybe this makes sense and maybe it's just dumb.

I'm sorry to be grumpy. It's unforgivable. I'm conflicted, that's the word. Here is what I need to find out: Is there something waiting to be said about nature in the nearby places? Can you learn what neighborhood nature has to teach, too—its weather patterns and English ivy, the moss in the eaves, the curbside gardens and blue tarps? Can a person live in town and write "true and fresh and natural" words—Thoreau again—with "earth still adhering to their roots"? Are town-dwelling nature writers oxymorons? Or worse, fakes? This is pretty important for somebody like me to know.

To get my annual dose of wildlands, I commute each summer to Pine Island, a dreamy tide-washed island in a hidden inlet. It's *very, very* wild, as "wild" is measured by the odds of being drowned or eaten by bears. I wish we could build a cabin there, because I'd like some protection at least from the rain, but that wouldn't be exactly legal. So we camp, as I've said, arranging our cook kit on the enormous log we call the kitchen and pitching a tent in the bedroom—a tangle of moss and roots.

But commuting to a treasured unpeopled place to write on summer vacations—what sense does that make? To get to this wild island takes the following: one Ford Expedition SUV trailering one 22-foot fiberglass boat with a 200 horsepower outboard motor and an 8 horsepower Evinrude, and a skiff with a 5 horse-power Mitsubishi outboard. Two motel nights each way. Twenty-six hundred miles, total; 212 gallons of gas—162 for the SUV, 50 for the boats. A gift of $402.80 to the oil industry. Frank and I can pretend this level of consumption does no harm to the earth, but it does, and to people who probably could put this amount of money to better use. So I don't know what to do.

The awful possibility is—okay, I'll just say it—Thoreau may have set sort of a bad example when he moved to the woods to live deliberately. It's not so much that he built the cabin—thousands of his compatriots were doing the same thing back then—as it is the reasons he gave, implying that moving to the woods (physically or meta-phorically?) is the way (the only way?) to live what actually is (biological or spiritual?) life, to live deep and suck out the marrow. Not like ants, he says, poor dumb ants, and I'm suspicious he's talking about me.

How would the world be different if Thoreau had lived with the Emersons and visited Walden Pond on Sundays, instead of the other way around? Would his prose be any less outrageous and astonishing? I'm not sure, but I'm fairly confident that fewer people would be moving to the mountains, or building their dream cabins by ponds, crowding out the coots in the land of ten thou-sand lakes and a hundred thousand lakeside cabins.

I'm not being fair. It's a good thing to make a home in a beautiful, sparsely populated place, and I'll list the reasons: One, because people defend their homes with uncommon ferocity, and defending beautiful, sparsely populated places is a good and necessary thing. Two, if nature writing is a good thing that has good effects—which it is, and does—and if living close to the land nurtures good nature writing—which it certainly has done—then the benefits of living and writing in the wild outweigh the harms.

But most of all, reason number three, some people are happier living in unpeopled places, and how can that be wrong? "Your morale improves; you become frank and cordial, hospitable and single-minded." I see this in myself, suspicious in town, grown cramped and white and infinitely divided, like pot-bound subterranean roots. On the weekends, I burst out of the city, gulping pure air, leaping about to press my face into juniper thickets and snowberry leaves, and my life blows open like a mountain sky. Complexities—a wire snare in the city—become, in the wilds, infinitely beautiful possibilities. Ideas clarify themselves. I grow close to the people with me. With my boots in decaying hemlock duff or intertidal muck, I grow happy. So okay.

But sometimes (just sometimes) I wish my writer friends would come back to the towns they left behind when it all got too crowded and sad. We know how beautiful the uninhabited places can be, and how precious, but what about the rest? When writers move away because they can't stand the bare-ass hills, they make people think you *can* leave destruction behind. When they write about nature out there, it becomes that much harder to remember the nature nearby. I know that Gertrude Stein complained that, in Oakland, "there's no there there." But it's equally true that no matter how far you go, "there's no away away."

Sometimes I think I might call up my writer friends who have moved out of town. Come home, I would say, and write about the clear-cut hillsides and the halogen-faded nights. Come home and write about the logging families fighting for the right to destroy their own livelihoods, or the virtual reality of children blinking on and off in video arcades. Fight for the close-in places as you fight for what is wild and good. Show your faithful readers that it's possible to connect deeply and meaningfully to the land, without living by the pond. Show them it's possible to suck the marrow out of life in the dry, brittle bones of the towns. Isn't this also a worthy calling?—to learn to live deliberately in neighborhoods while there are still a few essential facts left. And to remember, when we come to die, that in whatever place we have lived, we have lived in the natural world.

NUTS AND GRUBS
(THE PRACTICAL BASIS
OF TRUST)

I WAS SITTING IN THE BACKYARD, drinking wine. It
was the second glass, but I'd spent all day grading mid-
terms, so I make no excuses. I'd started reading the newspaper, but the headlines depressed me. Enron, Worldcom,
corporations stealing from each other, from the stock-
holders, the customers. Wars for oil, gold. Disgusting.
So I was sitting there tossing Sociables onto the lawn.
Sociables are crackers: lots of oil and some seeds, which,
I guess, is about as sociable as anything else these days.

Frank has told me that scrub jays don't come in for
food in the fall; that it's too late in the season, that their
babies are fledged and they don't need all the extra calories. But if I wanted to toss crackers to the scrub jays, I
guessed I would, and if they didn't eat them, the crackers
would melt in the rain that was forecast for the next day. I
squinted at the small print on the package: 50 calories per

serving, serving size, 3 crackers. Tossing out the crackers
would save me the calories anyway.

A jay fussed around in the garden, over in the bark
dust next to the grape arbor. He had something in his
beak, something dark and round, but I couldn't make
it out, and I couldn't go into the house for binoculars
without scaring him, so there you have it. He was looking over his shoulder, as if he were nervous, and eyeing
the ground. I mean, literally, eyeing. He took an eye and
pointed it to the ground. Then he pointed his other eye
to the ground. I think it would be awful to have to con-
sult both eyes, to let each one draw its own conclusion and
then debate. Yes. No. There's enough uncertainty in my life
already: I don't need my eyes to act like jerks, each insist-
ing on its own point of view. Anyway, the debate must
have been inconclusive, because the jay hopped to another
place with his mouth full, and eyed it anew.

In the meantime, a second jay was watching from the
rhododendron. I didn't know whether to alert the first jay
or not. But the issue quickly became moot, because the
second jay, the interloper, cried his murder cry.

If you don't live in jay country, you probably haven't
encountered the murder cry. I've heard it only a few
times myself. It must be *A Nightmare on Elm Street* to a
jay. Freddy with the knife-blade fingers, or whatever—
I'm not a big movie fan. The interloper jay bobbed up
and down, as if its legs were accordion springs. Up and
down. And it made this special call. Like a playing card
stuck with a clothespin to a bike wheel spinning really

fast. Like somebody running a stick along a picket fence. Wooden. Like wood gargling.

The first time I heard the murder cry, the crier had swooped down, hawk-style, and attacked another jay. This was a serious avicidal attack. They grasped each other with their claws and hacked at each other with their beaks until I finally went over and said this is not civilized, guys, and cut it out. Which they did. Sometimes you have to take charge in your own back-yard.

So the second jay made this murder cry. And the first jay took whatever he had in his beak—I was starting to think it was a hazelnut—hopped under the grape arbor, and poked the nut into the dirt. Then he jabbed it with his beak and flew away.

Long pause.

The second jay swooped in to the hiding place, poked his beak into the ground, and came up with the nut. He looked in all directions.

This was a theft. I was witnessing a theft.

Then that jay scuttled across the yard holding the prize in his beak, looking guilty. First, you will say, jays don't scuttle. Okay, it was hopping; but it looked like scuttling because there was no flying involved, and he was running sort of hunched down, like he was trying to make himself small.

And maybe you are thinking, well, it wasn't exactly *theft*, maybe unauthorized *possession* or something, be-cause it's probably in the *nature* of a jay to take things,

built into what a jay *is,* and you can't say he decided to
steal the other guy's food. It's just the way he's *made,*
and it's not like there's some *moral agent* to blame
behind those eyes. And what are you going to do?—
put him in jail?

But don't start making excuses. I saw what I saw.
And don't tell me jays don't feel guilty. This jay stopped
in the middle of the yard, looked to one side, looked to
the other (the arguing eyes), hopped some more, quickly,
quickly, to the cover of a squash plant. Okay, so maybe
that wasn't guilty. But he was definitely stealthy. (You
might be resisting my pronouns by this point, but
this is male behavior. Sorry, but I don't think this is
a woman jay, running off with the booty.) So, he ran
like a sniper from hiding place to hiding place, all the
way through the flower garden and down the driveway
(behind the front tire, behind the rear tire, behind a rose
bush). Finally he was in the rose garden and now *his* eyes
started to take charge. The right eye examined the place
in the pigweed behind the rose. The left eye examined
the same place. They had a discussion. He looked over
his shoulder.

I was hiding behind the van, having left my chair and
my wine to see where he was going to hide this hazelnut. I don't think he saw me. He poked the nut into the
ground. Then he fired up his beak, which must be one
tough piece of bird, and gave the nut a couple of good
whacks to drive it into the ground. Then he looked all
around, over his shoulder, probably checking the neighborhood for other murder-jays, maybe a rival gang.

Moving quickly, he picked up a dried rose petal and put it on top of the cache. Then a dried-up, black-spot mottled rose leaf. He gave it all another whack. Then, quickly: three more rose petals. Did he think that nobody was going to notice this? Of course, in my garden, probably nobody *would* notice a pile of shed leaves and used-up petals. But from my vantage point behind the left wheel well of my van, it looked like a cache.

My neighbor came out of her back door heading for her garbage cans. Unfortunate timing: blundering into the scene of the crime while the crime is in progress. The right eye took a last look and the bird flew into the trellis above a dead Cecile Brunner rose. He hopped up, up, onto the last rung, and sat in what was left of the sun. As if no crime had been committed. As if he were born again, clean and sweet as a baby. As if the first jay wouldn't come back some hungry day, maybe starving, the perfect memory in his little brain expecting a nice hazelnut 3 inches SE 140 degrees from the grape arbor, and find nothing.

The thief looked over his shoulder at my neighbor. Then he swooped down and dug up the nut with a few flicks of his beak. He hopped the length of the garden, quickly rehid the nut under the root of an azalea, and flew away.

So here is the most amazing thing Frank told me. Jays that steal from other jays are more likely to be suspicious that other jays will steal from them. A scientist named Nicola Clayton took two groups of birds—some of the jays had pilfered grubs from their comrades, others had not. When the thief-jays buried a grub while another bird was watching, they snuck back later, dug up the grub, and hid it in a new place. But the trustworthy jays were trusting; they didn't bother to re-hide their grubs. It probably never occurred to them that a jay would steal.

So how can anybody read the newspaper and not be exasperated? It's not that tough to figure out. If you take more than your fair share, people aren't going to trust you—why should they?—or come to your defense. And (the lesson of the birds) if you take more than your fair share, you're certainly not going to trust other people; you know from firsthand experience how underhanded some people can be. So you're always nervous and defensive, and what kind of life is that?

To keep hold of what you've taken, to protect yourself from attackers, real or imagined, you have to defend yourself. The gated community, the fancy electric locks on the Lexus, the private school, the security guards, the tasteful pistol, the troop carrier, the nuclear arsenal. But this takes serious money. So you accumulate more and more, hiding what you're doing, denying even the concept of "one's fair share," undercutting anybody's reason to trust you. That creates enemies, and sure: you should be afraid of them. And so it goes.

I walked over to the azalea and dug up the purloined hazelnut. Carrying it back to the grape arbor, I reburied it there, where its original owner might find it come winter. It's going to be a full-time job, keeping track of all the nuts and grubs. But like I say, sometimes you have to take charge in your own backyard.

BLOWING THE DAM

WHEN FRANK AND I bought the land that straddles
the Marys River, included in the deal was a little dam
that blocked the river bank-to-bank. The Marys is a
small river that empties into the Willamette River from
the hills west of town. It's barely a creek by Oregon
standards. The dam wasn't much of a dam either, just
a three-foot-high concrete wall built by a farmer to
power the paddle wheel for his private electrical plant.
By the time we bought the land, the farmer had moved
on, the pastures had grown up to Queen Anne's lace
and bracken, and the paddle-wheel blades had rusted
off and washed downriver. But the dam remained. We
decided to blow it up.

Even though it was insignificant as dams go, our dam
made life hard for Willamette River cutthroat trout. At
high water, the cutthroats could migrate over the dam to
the feeder streams to spawn. The problem came at low
water, just when the river started to warm up and the fish
were heading downstream again to cooler, deeper water.
Then, our dam blocked the Marys, forcing the fish to

hang out in warm slack water, waiting for rain. The dam blocked canoeists, too, who had to portage through a wicked blackberry bramble or jump out of their boat, haul it across the dam, and climb in again — tricky stuff with a loaded boat. But what bothered me most, I guess, was the whole idea of somebody thinking that it was okay to stop a river, to silence it, to make it into something else, something muddy and useful to one person alone.

Taking out a dam wasn't a political issue ten years ago, and it never occurred to us that it might be a legal issue. Somebody put a dam in; somebody could take it out. As Frank and I talked it over, we didn't distinguish blowing up from taking out, breaching, or notching a dam. We just wanted to get the dam out of the way, and dynamite was good enough. The Yellow Pages are full of ads for people who blow things up for a living — Total Demolition Inc., Serving the Willamette Valley for Twenty-five Years. We made the arrangements and paid in advance.

A fist of concrete in the center of the road was the first sign of trouble when we drove to the river the day after the dam came out. Even before the river came into view, we could see rocks littering the roof of the neighbor's barn, and when we climbed through blackberries to the creek, we found rubble scattered everywhere. Twisted rebar stuck out of the river, each post catching a little V of twigs and dried leaves. The guys must have drilled some holes, stuck in the dynamite, lit a fuse, and run like hell.

We fell all over ourselves apologizing to the neighbors, but they were just grateful that by some blind miracle we hadn't brained their cow. Wading into the river, we started sawing out the rebar with the neighbors' hacksaw. It was a wet business, leaning over at the waist, up to our armpits in silty water, sawing away. The river was so muddy that we stumbled around, feeling with our feet for rubble, stopping sometimes to wiggle our tennis shoes loose from the silt. All afternoon, we hauled blocks of concrete out of the riverbed, arranging them as artfully as we could along the edge. Every time I stood to stretch my back I heard restless water and felt the awakening river push against my legs.

As hard we worked to clean the bed of the little reservoir, the river worked harder, lifting clouds of silt from the gravel and swirling them toward a beach at the bend downriver. By the end of the day, what had been slack water was a flowing stream again. Exhausted, we sat on the roots of a willow tree and watched the river, washed silver by a watery sun emerging between clouds and hills.

I wish I could say there were trout leaping in rainbow arcs over the river. I wish I could say there were trumpets. There were not. But from every rush and backwash, each swell of water over rock, each small spurt and riffle, each surge, all the slosh and spill of a river on the move, came a music we had never heard in that place.

Now, ten years after the Great Demolishment, the Marys runs strong across a riffle, hesitates, then dives in a smooth swell over the sill where the dam used to be. The piles of broken concrete are hard to see; moss and iris grow up between them and blackberry canes crawl over them in a tangled net. The banks still slough where the dam piled water against them, but some willows are beginning to take hold. The Marys has its problems—agricultural runoff from pastures upstream and clear-cutting on the highest hills. But cutthroat breed freely in the little streams upriver and, on a good day, the water runs clear under the roots of the willows.

Wronged and wronged again, the natural systems of the earth are gracious—giving us second chance after second chance, whether we deserve it or not. A salmon fighting its way upstream to spawn in water muddied by cows is a gift of grace. Alders that grow up green in bare-dirt clear-cuts are gifts of grace, and so is fireweed. So are oil-eating bacteria and rain on city streets and sun through a hospital window. Marshes are all forgiveness, filtering fouled water, storing carbon dioxide and frog song, sheltering duck eggs, hiding the tiny, fleeing fishes. And a river is an agent of forgiveness, cutting channels through the silt, building islands, watering the willows that will hold its banks.

But retribution is built into the systems of the earth, too, when an act carries its own punishment. A landslide that thunders down the steep, denuded slope, lifting the screams of crows and burying the villages. A tuna that seeds mercury in the brain of the man who gaffs it. Farmlands that hide pesticides in the dark soil to poison the next generation of children, all the sins of the fathers visited on their sons.

An earth that is at once functionally forgiving and thunderously vengeful raises all the familiar questions of redemption and remorse. When it comes to the earth, can there be redemption in good works?

❦

IN THE UPPER REACHES of the Marys River, one of my friends is growing a grandfather forest. The primeval forest on his forty acres burned in the Burnt Woods fire in 1850. Loggers cut the few trees that survived. When the forest finally grew back to tall trees a hundred and thirty years old, loggers felled it again. My friend's calling is to recreate the giant, mossy-backed, dim-lighted forest of trees that once lived and died in this place. Scientists told him it takes five hundred years for a forest to reach this ripeness, but the news seems not to have discouraged him.

Each winter, he and his wife order hundreds of little seedlings tied in bundles. Loading them in soaked burlap bags, they troop over the hills, planting trees as they believe the trees would have planted themselves: A spindly hemlock seedling on a decaying stump. A wide sweep of western red cedars on the rainward side of a hill. A Douglas-fir next to the creek, and a huckleberry in its shadow. No regular rows with six-foot centers, no cloned siblings in rank. The man and his wife cast an eye over the landscape, choose a sheltering place, thwack the hoedad into the soft soil, heave back on the handle to make a small hole, poke in a seedling, pull it up just a touch to straighten the roots, and tamp it down where it can grow for five hundred years.

When spring comes and skunk cabbage starts to bloom in the beaver marsh, they pull on black rubber boots and go out to *release* the trees. This is a word of the forester's art—to release, to set free from constraint, like a once-caged bird. They kneel by a tiny tree and pull away the matted layer of winter leaves. Soft green fronds spring up. In a good year, the leaders on a Douglas-fir may grow a foot; three feet in a very good year.

When the man and his wife die, time and the forest will take up the work where they left off. In two hundred years, a wind storm may fell the tallest trees. Moss will blanket them where they shatter in the scattered shadows of vine maples. In three hundred years, the biggest trees will be ten feet across, and their roots will tangle in the dark with bacteria and the white threads of fungi. In four hundred years, lichens will hang from every limb and licorice ferns will grow from the branches. The moss and vine maple, the bacteria and fungi, even the windstorm itself, are gifts of grace and rebirth. In five hundred years, the forest will be filled with forgiveness the way a forest fills with light, evidence that wrongs against the forest have been forgotten and life goes on.

D. Elton Trueblood, who once taught philosophy at Earlham College, wrote that a person "has made at least a start on discovering the meaning of life when he plants shade trees under which he knows full well he will never sit." I've been thinking about this. That they have the power to forgive, to make themselves whole again, says a great deal about the great ecological systems. But

Trueblood's point is important too: it says a great deal about human beings, that they put their backs to the hard, unending work of trying to undo the harms done to the world—not for their own sakes, but for the sake of the world and the well-being of people they will never meet. This is the work of redemption.

Maybe the meaning of life will turn out to be a verb, something one does, some work, some endless process, rather than an end-state. Maybe its tools are hoe-dads and dynamite, and a person can find the meaning of life on the very day she's wearing big black rubber boots and an embarrassing rain hat. Maybe human beings will find their purpose, their reason for being, in planting trees, releasing trees, breaching dams, releasing rivers—as the forests and rivers are reborn, finding their own rebirth and release in the good hard work of hope.

LAST WEEK I DROVE down the Marys to the Willamette, and down the Willamette to the stair-stepped reservoirs that northwesterners still affectionately call the Columbia River. On the east side of the Cascade Range, this is scabland, a steppe of sage and bunchgrass prairies, layer on layer of basalt laid down by lava flows and shaped by floods into brown velvet hills, greening in the creases on this spring day, capped with fraying clouds and scalloped with rimrock and high-tension wires from hydro-electric plants. At the place where the river once turned on edge and thundered between basalt cliffs, where

native people stood on platforms and hauled salmon
from the maelstrom in long-handled nets, where in
March 1957 the floodgates of the Dalles Dam closed
and a reservoir drowned the river overnight, I stood on
the lawn by the water and tossed pieces of my McBreak-
fast to a gull. The noise was deafening—roaring trucks on
the highway, bells at the railroad crossing, and then the
rapid pulse of an empty train. The river itself was silent.

I don't know when this dam will go—or by what process, natural or political. But someday, it will be removed.
Sitting in my car behind a chain-link fence that separates
the highway from the river, I can imagine people lined
up at the edge of the Columbia on the day the Dalles
Dam is breached and the riverbed rises slowly into
that blue desert air. Water pours from every crease, and
smooth basalt slabs appear, gray and mammoth. People
will pull into the highway overlooks, stand in small
groups under cottonwoods in the riverside parks, wade
across the mud to pile stone cairns at the falling edge of
water—crowds of people, gathering quietly to witness the
rebirth of a river.

In the first days, all they will hear is a whisper, the
movement of silt in warm water. But as the lake falls away
and a rocky island splits the channel, the river will shout
over rapids and then begin to roar, a full-throated roar lifting the screams of gulls and the laughter of children who
jump from rock to rock, leaving their footprints in soft
sand beside the prints of geese, scooping minnows from
pools of water stranded inside rotting tires.

Maybe the people will cheer. Maybe they will pray. Maybe they will weep when they see the pale riverbed, drowned for a very long time. But the first rain will clean the highest rocks, the first flood will cut a channel through the silt. Storksbill and balsam root will poke up between slabs of mud drying on new riverbanks, and I know from experience that there will come a time when the roots of willows will reach into clear water again.

FIRE AND WATER

I'D ALWAYS THOUGHT that when I died, my children
would scatter my ashes under the pines beside Davis
Lake, where we have camped for twenty years. But it's
all ashes there now. Wildfire flared up along the road
behind the east campground. Driven by 25-mile-an-hour
winds, the firestorm charged across the road and ran hard
and fast through miles of lodgepole pines, torching the
manzanita and exploding into the crowns of the trees.
Fire crews pulled back and let it burn; what else could
they do with the fire roaring around them?

For two weeks, heavy smoke and unpredictable winds
closed the roads into Davis Lake. Helpless, I watched on
the Internet as the fire expanded, red spots encircling the
lake until the whole map was blotchy red. But as soon as
fire crews cleared the trees that had fallen across the road
and removed the barricades, I headed for Davis Lake,
driving the Cascades Highway through a healthy forest
of ponderosa pines.

Car windows down, I could smell the thick beds of
pine needles, warm and sweet in the sun. Ponderosas

rose from meadows of green grass, blue sagebrush, currants already turning orange. Then suddenly the color was gone. For miles in front of me, all I could see was a blanket of white ash stuck through with tree trunks, broken and black, and the shadow of a raven swerving between spars. A thin line of smoke rose from a smoldering stump. I pulled into an overlook on the side of the road, stepped into ashes, and listened.

I had loved the sound of Davis Lake in the spring. I remember waking early one morning, years ago, under pines at the edge of the lake. As Frank and our little ones breathed quietly beside me, great blue herons flapped over the marshland, croaking. Red-breasted nuthatches called from the pines. Coots splashed in circles, and sandhill cranes clattered on the far side of the lake, leaping and flapping their wings in a clumsy dance. I remember how the frogs shouted that morning, filling the air like a cheering crowd. In a pine far down the lake, fledgling eaglets begged without ceasing, a scraping sound like pebbles against steel. I settled deeper in my sleeping bag, warm and grateful.

But now the silence was so complete that I brushed my ears to be sure I could still hear. Finally a raven called. A single grasshopper scratched in black stubble. The wind lifted slender whirlwinds from the ashes. But without pine needles to make music of the wind, even the whirlwinds were silent. I stood with my head back and my eyes closed, trying to understand how it could be so suddenly gone— the green singing life of this place.

I'm a philosopher by trade, so I should know how to be philosophical about loss. The world is in flux, and change is the only constant. Forests are no exception; they grow and burn and grow again. I know this. Everybody knows it. Almost three thousand years ago, the Greek philosopher Heracleitus acknowledged the necessity of change: You can't step into the same river twice, he said. But why not, I want to know. Why can't what is beautiful last forever?

Everything has to change, Heracleitus answers, because all the world is fire and water in constant conflict. Fire advances and is quenched by water. Water floods and is boiled away by fire. And so people wake and sleep, live and die, the fires of their spirits steaming against the dampness of their flesh. Summer changes into winter, as sun gives way to rain. The mountains boil up from the seas, and the seas come into being and pass away. Forests are reduced to ashes, and from the ashes rise new forests, damp and shining.

How easy it is to write these words, so good in theory. But in fact, the only thing rising from the ashes today are the whirlwinds. A pickup rumbles into the overlook. A man steps out, inhales sharply, then turns to his buddy. "Look at those huge big dirt devils," he says. The two of them stand without speaking, watching ashes lift in thin spiraling threads and flatten against the sun.

❦

ONE AUGUST EVENING maybe fifteen years ago, Frank and I crouched on the beach with our children, thrilled and terrified. We flinched each time lightning struck the forested ridge three miles across Davis Lake. A thunderous crack, a flash of light that turned our eyelids blue. Then a flame flickered on the ridge and a thin tendril of smoke rose into the air. Lightning struck into the forest again and again until the hillside was dotted with little flames, each with its trail of smoke, like candles on a birthday cake.

Over our shoulders, the moon rose, flaky and red. The lightning moved slowly away over the lava ridge, flashing silently above the eastern plains. Frank tucked the children into their sleeping bags, then sat by the tent, watching across the lake. I launched a canoe onto water that pooled red around my bow. Every pull of my paddle spun off a ruddy spiral and vibrated the lake into red and purple ripples. I could smell smoke and water, damp algae on the shore. Gradually, as I rocked in my boat, black clouds drifted over the face of the moon, and water licked in the reeds. Soft rain fell, ticking on water that faded from red to gray, and one by one, those fires went out.

Water won that round. But I knew that fire's time would come.

For eighty years, lodgepole pines have grown up thick as dog hair on the flats around Davis Lake. A person deliberately laying a fire in that forest couldn't have done a better job than the trees did themselves. Pile kindling under each tree—stacks of downed branches, hard and silver and scratchy. Sprinkle the kindling with dry pine needles. Drape branches into the kindling so any ground fire is sure to climb the tree. Let the forest bake in the sun and the drying wind. Then all it takes is a spark—dry lightning, a Bic lighter, an ATV.

Lodgepole pines need to burn. It's the earliest science lesson I remember.

When I was growing up in Cleveland, somebody mailed my father a shoebox crammed with lodgepole pine cones. Although he had never seen a lodgepole forest, he had read of these western trees in biology books and the journals of Lewis and Clark. So as my sisters and I jostled around him, he spread the cones on a cookie sheet and baked them in the oven. We watched through the oven door, marveling as the cones bloomed like roses in the heat, releasing papery seeds.

My father handed each of us a seed, and together we admired this wonder: how the cones stay on the trees for years, tight as fists, until fire warms the resin that holds them shut and they release the seeds to replant the burned-out forest—a forest made in just such a way that the very fire that destroys it will create it anew.

So I can understand the battles between water and fire, cycles of living and dying, the urgent necessity of death, all of us designed to die—just exactly that—everything we love designed to die, as the lodgepole pine forest is made to burn. I can understand this in my mind, but how will understanding ease this loss?

DAVIS LAKE HAS ALWAYS been a lesson in the cycles of living and dying. One year, the water in Davis Lake rises so high it floods into the trees. In a year like that, the whole valley shimmers—a gleaming bowl, alive with trout and mayflies. Another year, the water is so low that the creek winds almost a mile across a playa to the clouded eye of the shrunken lake. Fishermen call each other to find out the lake level. "Where's Davis Lake this year?" they ask. It's always a disappointment when the lake's too low to launch a boat, but the water always comes back.

Last week, I called my friend Allen Throop to find out how a natural lake can overflow one year, almost disappear the next, and then reappear a year later, calm and glistening, as if nothing had happened. Allen is a geologist, and how he wishes he had been there when Davis Lake formed. First there was just a broad valley cut by a creek fed by a thousand tiny springs. Then the valley heaved and lava poured out, crackling across the path of the creek. He wishes he could have seen the plumes of steam and heard the thunderous rock, the creek water stopping the lava in its tracks, the lava plugging up the creek, the titanic battle between fire and water, played out right here 5,500 years ago, long before Heracleitus walked the streets of Ephesus.

Snow falls on the mountains above Davis Lake, melts, and trickles through the porous rock, making its way— maybe in a matter of months, maybe in a year—through the mountain to the springs that feed the lake. But as water pours into Davis Lake, water flows out through the lava dam and lake bed. The depth of the lake depends on how much water flows into the lake, and how much water percolates through the lava dam or drains through the cracked lake floor.

At shallow water, you can see the funnels, the "suck holes," my family calls them, where water spirals into cracks in the lava, like water down the drain. I've floated in a canoe over these funnels, looked through to where the water goes from blue to turquoise, to indigo, then disappears in midnight black, the shades of color deeper as the water swirls away. This terrifies me, to float above the place where water drains into prehistoric darkness and a silence unbroken and complete, as if the silence could suck a person down before she's ready to go.

You can say that it's all a natural process, that the appearances and disappearances are all the result of cycles working themselves out over time. A lodgepole pine forest isn't merely the place that shelters my tent; it's a process of growth and change—trees transforming themselves to ashes to green seedlings to barren spars to seeds on the wind. The lake isn't only a place where my children float with blue dragonflies. It's a stream of water that flows from light on the mountaintops to the long, dark caves, emerging into the blue lake and plunging into the dark again like a serpent that has no end. And what is a human life but a new arrangement of molecules that once were stars?

You can say that it's something particularly human: this tendency to misunderstand natural change as unsupportable loss. You can say that sorrow is part of the same arrogance, the same self-centeredness that leads humans to measure time by the span of their own lives, to define what is real by their own needs.

If I could step outside my own life span and purposes, then maybe I could make myself believe that the difference between a natural disaster and a natural cycle is only a matter of time. Aldo Leopold advised his readers to think like a mountain—on that timescale. A mountain wouldn't mourn the loss of a forest any more or less than a human mourns the leaves that twist off an oak in autumn.

But how can I think like a mountain? Tell me: Does a mountain feel its scree slipping to its feet, or hear sand sliding ceaselessly down its flank?

ALL THE BACK ROADS into Davis Lake were closed by barricades and striped tape. But the assistant fire manager for the Deschutes National Forest, Gary Morehead, agreed to drive me in. I pulled on the yellow, fire-resistant suit he handed me. Then he shoved his truck into gear and steered it around the first barricade.

We followed a dusty track through a landscape of black tree trunks stuck at every angle to the ashes. Here was where cats bulldozed a clearing in the forest, Gary told me, a safety zone where firefighters could retreat if the flames turned on them. Here was where the force of the fire-generated wind snapped every tree and sent it crashing into flames. The truck bumped down to the site of the campground, next to the creek that fed the lake. As I stepped out of the truck, my feet lifted smudges of dust.

There in the ashes was a fire ring, solid and ironic, and the bent frame of a lawn chair, tossed on its head. A sign that once pointed to the boat landing was reduced to a bolt stuck through a post burned to a spindle.

The fire created a wind so fierce, Gary said, that it threw a canoe into a tree, and drove flames against it until the canoe melted over the branches. When the branches burned away, all that remained was a metal frame collapsed against what was left of the trunk. The fire vaporized two spotted owl nests; too young to fly, the owls surely died. And the firestorm sucked the eagles' nest out of the tree.

I trudged along the edge of the lake. Where, in ashes turned violet by the ferocity of the fire, was the place where I laid on pine needles with our newborn son, pointing out yellow-rumped warblers and chickadees? I wanted to find the shallow reed bed where Jonathan, grown into a toddler, waded after minnows; before we could convince him to leave the water, his legs were streaked with leeches. I wanted to find the place where Erin wove tule reeds into a little cubbyhole, crawled in, and read Dr. Seuss, tracking the words with her finger. Could it be here, in this empty space, that Frank and I drank wine at a picnic table, talking about our kids gone off to college, until stars popped out, spangling in the pines like lights on a Christmas tree?

One year this ground was covered with toads. Another year, it was baby garter snakes and buttercups. Now, the ground was covered with black stubble burned right to the water. I stood beside the cove where Frank and I rode the canoe back to shore on a windy day, streams of light and water hitting our faces. I remembered the cool wind, the bucking canoe, the exhilaration, the wheeling eagles, but all I could see was the lake calmly reflecting the devastation of this place, just sitting there, as if all that life—all those precious, irreplaceable times—hadn't roared into flames and vanished forever.

I ASKED GARY IF WE could go to the headwaters of Ranger Creek, where I remembered a spring that flowed out of the mountainside and made its way through flowered meadows to Davis Lake. He was reluctant to go there, not sure if the place had been secured. But he circled the truck around the yellow tape and brought us slowly through the ashes to what was once a willow flat at a bend in the creek.

I was surprised by what I saw. Stumps still smoldered, two weeks after the fire. But already, new grass had grown four inches high, green as frogs. The willow thickets had burned down to blackened stubs that reached up like a hand extending from the ground, the black fingers as short as my own. But inside each hand, as if spiraling from a wound in the palm, was new growth, the coiled leaves unfurling. There were birds there, osprey, soaring over the water, watching for trout.

The springs surged from the barren ground into a burst of green, shimmering and miraculous in that field of gray. Trees had fallen over the creek and burned in from both ends, but between the banks, the tree trunks were intact, shading the water, shaded themselves by tall green rushes. Wherever water reached into the ashes, plants grew—rosy spirea, cinquefoil yellow as buttercups, and sweet bracken fern.

What is this world, that it has all these things?—the dead and dying forest, the charred bones of young owls, and water pouring from the earth, ancient snow finally emerging again and flowing into the great expanse of blue. What is this world, that life and death can merge so perfectly that even though I search at the edge of water, I can't find the place where death ends and life begins?

I was standing there, in all my color, the blue veins in my elbows, the reddened skin on my knuckles, my fireman's yellow suit; standing there in all my noise, the breath in and out, the wind flapping my collar. But some day my children would bring my ashes, gray and silent, to be caught up in a dirt devil that makes no noise at all. And where will the color be then, and the sound of a person breathing? This silence, so hard to understand.

In Heracleitus's world of constant change, don't we all yearn for some pause in the river, an eddy, where the water slows and circles back upstream for a long, calm time before it rejoins the flow? This is what Davis Lake was for me—a quiet circle of the seasons, a place where the world seemed to come to rest. A place my family could return, year after year, as the cranes returned, as the water returned, and the yellow blooms of the bitterbrush. The constancy of the lake had reassured me, the reliable circle of life.

But in this greening place of ashes and springs, I began to understand that time cannot move in a circle, coming again to where it was before. Time sweeps in a spiral, going round and round again—the cycles of the seasons, the flow of the cold springs, the growth of a forest or a child, but never returns to the same place.

And shouldn't I be grateful for this? That birds will nest in the Davis Lake basin, even though that particular pair of owlets will never fly again. Trees will grow beside the creek, as my grandchildren will grow on the green-banked stream. Willow thickets will tremble with morning ice, the songs of red-winged blackbirds, the slow unfolding of a dragonfly's wings. And we who love this world will tremble with the beauty of the spiral that has brought us here and the mystery of the spiral that will carry us away.

FOUR AUTUMN STORIES

I. GARDEN GERANIUM
(Pelargonium hortorum)

I WAS OUT EARLY on a foggy October morning,
snapping the heads off geraniums beside my garage. I
trimmed the chrysanthemums to the ground, piling
dead leaves in a mound over their roots. The petunias
had grown rangy, so I pulled them out and tossed them
in the yard debris bin. With a sharp tug, I separated
gladiolus leaves from their bulbs, leaving a raw place.
I'll dig the bulbs with a pitchfork when the soil dries a
little, throw away the rotten ones, and replant the biggest bulbs along the south wall of the house.

My roses were struggling. The few rosebuds still
on the bushes strove against long odds—low fog, temperatures in the forties, and a bubbling sheen of aphids.
Bushtits and chickadees swarmed over the bushes,

gorging themselves. I crushed aphids between my thumb and forefinger until my fingertips were green and slick.

The books say to stop deadheading roses in October so they can set hips, a process that somehow signals them to settle in for the winter, to stop trying so hard, to put energy into their roots and let flowering go for another year. My body was setting hips too, so I had mixed feelings about the roses. The temptation was to give them another shot of fish emulsion, tell them to buck up, give it another try, take risks. Maybe winter will come late. Maybe there will be time for another round.

I hacked away at the evergreen clematis. It is a horror show of a plant, growing at jungle rates, pulling itself along the ground like an animal with a broken back, crawling up a holly tree and engulfing its crown. But I didn't know quite what to think about this, because it was the neighbors' holly that had been engulfed, and I confess to uncharitable feelings toward the neighbors, who took a chain saw to the laurel hedge that shelters my backyard. But I pulled and chopped, as dead leaves and branches piled up around my feet. So near the end of the season, bitterness was one of the things I was trying to root out of my garden.

Garden advice columns in the morning newspaper implored me to compost my yard debris, but I wasn't sure. The neighbor worries that compost piles would smell and anyway, I'd come to believe that it isn't good to read garden advice columns in the fall. As morning temperatures drop and fog shrouds the maples, advice columns become more and more apocalyptic. Clear debris from your garden or viruses will incubate in rotting leaves and spread as a plague upon the land. Poison the slugs, mow the Saint-John's-Wort, dig the tubers, spray lime sulfur, the kingdom is at hand. Powdery mildew, fire blight, peach leaf curl, black spot, moth and rust, and maybe so.

But even as morning glories turned black and died around them, flower buds on the camellias had already grown as thick as thumbs and showed an edge of pink. Beneath them, tiny paired leaves carpeted the ground. They might have been lamb's-quarters, but then again, they might have been the start of forget-me-nots that would grow knee-deep by April. I gathered leaves that had blown onto the new plants and carried them to the disposal bin. Then I peeled off my gardening gloves and stretched my back. Forgiveness, forgetfulness, gentleness were in the fog that sank into the gardens in the morning, softening the colors—the vague light, the smell of rotting leaves, the relaxed, slept-in look of the rose beds.

II. MUSKGRASS CHARA
(Chara chara)

I USED TO LOVE ALL SMELLS. The smell of morning woke me smiling—air fresh as raw corn silk, cold in my nose. I loved the smell of clothes under a steam iron. Garlic baking. And the sea! I used to drive all the way to the beach just to breathe. My children would tease me.

"Ah, smell the fish-packing plants," they'd rhapsodize, but it was true: I loved the sopping, salty air along the bay front where conveyer belts pulled heaps of shrimp from the holds of trawlers, and the air was all creosote and iodine. And the smells of my children, different every year: Milk at first, and laundry detergent, then fresh grass from the neighbor's yard, pine sap and sewing machine oil, new textbooks, pears, and leftovers in lunchboxes, then perfume and a vague drift of cigarettes. Each friend's house had a different smell, and I knew without asking where my children had been.

Back then, there weren't any bad smells. But lately, I've been noticing the smells of my students. They smell of fresh air mostly, damp hair, damp wool, the great swig of outdoors that comes in the door with a student who's walked all the way across campus. But some of my students wear an unbearable aftershave; I think that's what it is. "I have an appointment across campus," I lie, "will you walk with me and we can talk." So we cross campus with our heads down, holding our coats against the weather, talking about Spinoza, while the rain washes the smell into the storm drains.

What I remember of childhood, of being frightened at night and coming into my parents' bedroom, is the molasses smell of people breathing all night in a closed room. When my father was sick, I remember his terror of odors, his fury at careless nurses, the sorrow as he became more and more body, less and less mind, until the body was all there was left, and it too started to effervesce, releasing its cells to the room. Then, I didn't want him to have any smell at all, except rain maybe, or outboard motors.

Now I can be obsessive about smells. Some days, I move through the house on a rampage. I throw out the sour beer bottles and wash the recycling bins with soap. I scrub the place where the wastebasket sits and set a fan to blow air out the basement window. When my children come home at Thanksgiving, I boil oranges with cinnamon and light a fire to pull stale air from the corners of the house. They will not come in the door and think, "This smells like an old house. I had forgotten how old."

And every October, I return to a lake that lies at the base of a great escarpment forested with ponderosa pines that smell like butterscotch pudding. In the evening, I take my kayak onto this lake. I sit alone in my boat, smacked by waves from an evening wind. As the sun begins to set, I can pick up a certain smell of water that reminds me of so many years and so many streams. It's a green alga, I think. Maybe *Chara*. If my father were alive, he could tell me the name. It's a green smell, a dense smell of water after the sun has gone behind the mountains.

I paddle to the line where the mountain's shadow is moving across the lake, then slowly paddle with the shadow as it advances toward the eastern shore. This is where the scent lifts off the water, just where the night is covering the day. Nighthawks dive low over the water. Redwings call. I paddle just fast enough to keep up with the advancing edge of shadow, just fast enough to keep pace with the turning of the earth.

III. DEER MOUSE
(Peromyscus maniculatus)

SEVERAL YEARS AGO, Frank and I lived all of
October in a cabin on the edge of a little lake. It had
been a drought year. Below the boathouse, we could see
rocks that no one had seen for some time. The birch
leaves fell early, yellow and brittle, and the cattail marsh
dried to cracked pans. And so of course we expected our
well water to taste like water at the bottom of a well. We
boiled it to be sure it was safe, but drank it anyway, covering the foul taste with coffee and tea. When the pump
finally went dry, we lifted the lid of the well, looked into
the circle of stones, and found three dead mice—just
matted black hair and a sheen of grease floating on what
water there was left.

So I have tasted death. I have washed my hair in it,
stood with puddles of death around my feet and soaped
my body. I have boiled it for tea. I have poured it through
fresh-ground coffee and drunk it with toast. Death has a
sharp, dark taste. Boiled bark and aluminum cans might
taste like death—if the bark and the cans had been for a
long time under a layer of leaves and snow.

IV. SCARLET MAPLE
(Acer rubrum)

IN OUR NEIGHBORHOOD many years ago, there was a
lady with a stooped back and a shank of white hair that

fell over her face. Her back was so bent that she might have spent her life looking straight at the ground, except that she hooked her head up sometimes and by twisting it sort of sideways, she could see out across her lawn. She lived on the next block, so the children and I passed by her house every day on the way to the elementary school. We didn't see her much during the winter and spring. But in October, she was always in her garden, picking up leaves as they fell, one by one. A red leaf swayed to the ground. She stood with her head crooked up and watched it fall. Then, bent from the hips, she stepped over, picked it up, and carried it to a bushel basket on her front porch. If she spent all day at the job, she could stay ahead of the leaves, picking up one leaf, and then another.

Erin and Jonathan called her the Leaf Lady. "Good morning," they would say each day. But she must not have heard them, because she almost never looked up from her steady work. "Why doesn't she use a rake?" they would whisper when we had gone a discreet distance past her house. I honestly didn't know. You'd think it would break a person's back, reaching down, picking up a leaf, reaching down, picking up a leaf. But maybe her hands couldn't hold a rake, or maybe the angle was all wrong, with her bent back.

"Should we sneak over and rake her leaves?" the children would ask, and I didn't know the answer to that question either. Was it work, I wondered, picking up each leaf, or was it something different? "You can offer to

rake her leaves," I said, but they never did. Once after
a wind storm, a Boy Scout troop swooped into her yard,
spread out like commandos, and raked the grass clean
in fifteen minutes, piling leaves in the street for the city
sweeper. But that didn't seem to make any difference one
way or another, because she was out the next morning, as
she always was, waiting for the next leaf to drop.

That's the end of the story.

The Leaf Lady must have died, I suppose, or moved
to a nursing home and then died. In any event, after
she'd been gone for a long time, house painters came,
and then somebody else moved in. Our children left the
elementary school for the high school and then went on
to college. So I haven't had much occasion to walk by the
Leaf Lady's house, and no reason to think of her.

But one day last fall, I was on my knees in my garden,
pulling autumn leaves off the asters that were still giving
blooms, though not so many. Scarlet maple leaves had
drifted onto the heather, too, and I picked them off and
cleared them away from the stems. The varied thrushes
were whistling—odd, this close to winter—and the sun
glanced in sideways through the hedge. "I should get up
and get the garden rake," I said to myself. But I didn't.
I stayed on my knees, picking the leaves off one by one,
raking the soil with my fingers.

If I had used a bamboo rake, I could have collected
all the leaves in a few broad strokes. The soil would have
smoothed into parallel lines under my rake, and the
leaves would have bunched in front of the tines, and I

could have lifted the rake and dumped a whole rake load of leaves in the bin. Then I could have gone on to something else.

But what if all you want to do is pick up leaves? What if you want the autumn day to last as long as it can? What if you want to be in the day from the first chickadee in the morning until the neighbors' children rush shouting home from school with their lunch buckets and construction-paper projects sailing in their wakes? To be in the day until the sun goes so low it finally shines in your eyes, even when your spine pins your eyes to the ground?

Then, each falling leaf, each single leaf slowly falling, marks each moment passing, and you want to pick it up, and hold it in your hand, and be sure of it. Everyone's leaves are numbered, and nothing makes more sense than to gather them, one by one. There is something about the air in autumn, the coldness at the edge of warmth, something sweet and infinitely sad, the cold soil maybe, warmed by low sun, giving its smells straight into the air, sublimating from solid to spirit, transforming itself into something that can enter your body, something you can turn over in your mind: The warmth, the filtered light, the shouts of children, the cascading seasons, the tick of leaves falling one by one.

A COASTAL ISLAND

sacred / mundane

Geography

The sea stack stands in the Pacific Ocean just off Yaquina Head, a hilly cape on the Oregon coast. In shape, the sea stack is a hundred-foot high molar of rock, roughly flat and steep-sided. Trodden nests and shoulder-to-shoulder birds cover the island—gulls, cormorants, murres, pigeon guillemots. Under their feet is a thin layer of soil where puffins build tunnel nests. Palisades of broken basalt pillars line the cliff faces, each one white-washed by generations of birds. Rubble heaps up at the base of the cliffs, bashed by swells that roll in across an unbroken sweep of the Pacific and lift in rooster tails against the stone.

No human is permitted on the sea stack. It's a bird sanctuary. So visitors drive to Yaquina Head and walk from a paved parking lot to the barricaded cliff edge, where they can study the island hardly a hundred yards away. The headland is a place of "Stay on the path" signs and uniformed interpreters. But the sea stack is a wild and winged place, lifting and coming to rest, noisy with the crash of surf, the rumble of rocks in the rubble fields, and the shrieks and squawks of gulls.

However different they seem now, the sea stack and Yaquina Head are both part of the same flow of lava, the westernmost toe of basalt that flooded onto Pacific beaches from volcanoes at the Idaho-Oregon border. When the hot lava flow reached the edge of the sea, it sank through the sediments on the sea floor. The advancing edge cooled and slowed, but molten lava continued to flow in behind it, bulging upward to form a rocky thumb. Pounded by waves, softer stone gave way over time. So now, all that is visible of the great lobe of underwater lava is the mounded headland and the sea-stack island a stone's throw offshore.

THE SACRED AND THE MUNDANE

YAQUINA HEAD ON THE Oregon coast is never the same from one day to the next. One day, a northwest wind tears at your raincoat and packs your ears with sand, and black clouds back up against the land like trucks in a traffic jam, waiting their turn to rumble on shore and dump their load of rain. Another day, sun sizzles on salt steam rising from the mussel flats, making you squint. Or it's broken clouds and rainbows, the lighthouse rising white above billows of Scotch broom, blooming yellow. But on the day that made me really wonder, I couldn't see the island or the headland, only white fog, and wet grass underfoot.

Hoping to see across to the birds on the sea stack, I had hiked to the edge of Yaquina Head, right up to the chain-link fence that kept me off a narrow ledge dropping a hundred feet to the sea. I could hear surf breaking below and birds raucous and quarrelsome on the

1

sea stack just offshore, but fog completely obscured the island and all its invisible birds.

There was a thud and a rustle, and a Brandt's cormorant landed right at my feet, a glossy black, short-tailed, snake-necked sea bird with a wicked hook at the end of its beak. It looked at me and blinked an eye that was vivid marine blue. Then it fluttered its wings, stretched its neck, and revealed a throat of the same astonishing blue—there, in the cold Oregon fog, the transparent blue of tropical seas. It danced in the milky air, stretching its neck, rocking its head up and down, flashing blue light, staring at me with those blue eyes. So sudden and exotic, it might have been a vision from another world, but what moved me was the realization that it wasn't—it was from this world, sudden and exotic enough.

There are people who believe that there are two distinct worlds, the sacred and the mundane—a perfect world that exists in a place and on a plane beyond human knowing, and an imperfect world where we live out our daily lives. The sacred may touch down on a mountaintop now and then, or reveal itself through a thin place in time, but it is not of this world. The mundane, on the other hand, is material, ordinary, mute, present, and useful.

The mundane is said to have instrumental value—it's good as a means to some other end. Thus, sand, wind, water, seabirds become commodities, something you can consume or exchange for something else—sand for concrete, wind for electrical power, water for drinking, seabirds for lunch or human fascination. But the sacred is said to have intrinsic value. It is good in itself; it can't be traded away. Even if there were no humans left to make any use of the sacred at all, it would be better that it exist than not. It is, as Robinson Jeffers described the Pacific coast, "the heart-breaking beauty [that] will remain when there is no heart to break for it."

My friend Viola Cordova would never have made this distinction. She believed that the mundane is sacred, and the sacred is mundane, although if you pressed her, she'd admit that the words didn't make any sense to her. I'm starting to think she might be right, that all these careful distinctions between ordinary and extraordinary don't hold up.

I wish I could ask Viola about a man I met, a man who searched and searched for the sacred, and sure enough: One day, when he was walking on the beach, he heard a voice, loud and clear. "Stand here," it said, "and God will speak to you." The man stood—what else could he do? He stood for a very long time, shifting his weight from one leg to the other. His back stiffened up, a flock of brants flew down the trough between the breakers, the wind came up and died down, he zipped his jacket and unzipped it, and then he went home.

I don't understand what he hoped to hear. The cold wind, the ache in his legs—didn't these tell him what he needed to know? That he is alive in this place at this time, alive in the midst of all this life. That he is aware in the midst of all that is mysterious, every fact that might not have been and yet is. The blowing sand, the storm-driven waves, people bent to the wind are all cause for surprise and celebration.

Instead of bowing his head and waiting for instructions, what if he had lain on his back in the midst of the mussels, lain there with barnacles poking his scalp, felt—in the hollow rack of his ribs—the breakers pound against domed rock, listened to the far-away, sand-coated children shout and the sand fleas pop, exhaled into the echoing air, as all the while tide crept in around him and surf exploded closer and closer to his brain? Would that be lesson enough?

The mundane—the stuff of our lives—is irreplaceable, essential, eternal and changing, beautiful and fearsome, beyond human understanding, worthy of reverence and awe. The English word for this combination of qualities is "sacred." So I don't mind using that language, even though I'm less committed to the words than to the moral consequences: If the mundane is sacred, and the sacred is mundane; if there are not two worlds, but one, and it is magnificent and mysterious enough to shake us to the core; if this is so, then we—you and I and the man on the beach—ought to live lives of gladness and gratitude.

Then, every act of gratitude or gladness is a counter-force to those who would make the stuff of the earth into commodities only, as the writer Freeman House pointed out. Gladness lifts the material world out of the merely mundane and makes it wonderful, and reminds us that as we use the sacred stuff of our lives for human purposes, we must do so gratefully, with full hearts.

ONE NIGHT, OF THREE HUNDRED SIXTY-FIVE

WE STOOD IN THE SMOKE of a small fire and drank cold beers with our gloves on. In the dusk, tundra swans flashed white as they dropped to the water. There must have been hundreds of swans, a winter storm of swans, and equal numbers of Canada geese, all sounding off— swans doo-whooping, geese clattering, an occasional thump from a hunter's gun.

Frank and I had agonized over where to camp, clicking through weather Web sites, looking for one place in Oregon that wouldn't be blanketed with clouds in the middle of November. In the end, we gambled on the forecast for the Cascade Range: clear skies with patchy ground fog, temperatures in the low teens. We needed clear skies that night. We had come to see the Leonid meteor showers, when Earth plows through dust from an exploded comet, putting on a show that astronomers predicted would be the most spectacular in a thousand years.

As soon as we arrived at the meadow beside the lake,

we hauled our gear through dried reeds and grasses, looking for the very best place to put our bed. It didn't have to be dry or out of the wind, but it had to have a full view of the sky. On a rise a hundred yards from the little lake, with only one scraggly pine to block our view, we spread out ground cloth, foam pads, and sleeping bags, and tucked a nylon tarp around the whole sliding stack to keep off the frost. Then we hurried to collect firewood, prying it from the frozen ground.

In November, dusk is long and deceiving. The lake disappears first, then the ground, then the mountains, and soon enough the fire itself becomes just an optical illusion, all light and no heat and that's all you can see, the trembling coals and yellow toes of your own frozen boots. We kicked out the fire and groped our way to bed.

Using only the heat sucked out of your body, it takes a long, miserable time to warm a goose-down sleeping bag. There are two strategies here. One is to wiggle and wiggle, hoping the heat your exercise generates will warm the bag. The other is to hold perfectly still, concentrating every unit of heat in the fabric closest to your body. I wiggled and Frank held still and between the two of us, it took a long, long time to get warm. The birds were making a ruckus out on the lake, yelling and laughing as the night got colder and darker. We lay flat on our backs, watching the sky through the narrow slits between our hats and the bags pulled over our noses.

The sky filled with stars, but for the moment, they seemed to be staying in place. Every time I blinked, more stars appeared. "Somebody once said," I told Frank, "that since space is infinite and there are stars throughout space, the only reason the sky isn't paved with starlight is that light from the farthest stars is still on its way. Someday, when all that light finally gets here, the night will be solid starlight."

"Except for dark matter," Frank said, but I didn't care. The sky was making good progress toward infinitely starry, and I was getting sleepy.

When I woke up next, white fog covered the lake like milk. I could still see the mountains, and treetops poking out of the fog. But even as I watched, the air next to the ground around us gradually went milky until ground fog closed over us too, and we lay under a thin pool of damp white air. Our next chance to see this meteor shower would be November 2099. "Better start exercising and eating broccoli," Frank said, but suddenly a meteor catapulted the width of the sky. We could see it through the fog, fuzzy gold like a Christmas tree garland unaccountably come to life. After a long time, we saw another. And then one more, but we were sure we were missing most of them. We debated without much enthusiasm: Should we get up, hike to a cold car, and search for a place where the fog had cleared? But we were finally warm, and too comfortable, and we tucked down and went to sleep.

When Frank woke me several hours later, the night was clear and black. Bright streaks of light darted in all directions. The meteors looked like minnows to me, the way they darted and disappeared—sun-striped minnows startling and streaking off in a night-dark mountain lake—and I was at the bottom of the lake, cold currents eddying over my face. Frank counted one meteor every ten seconds, six a minute, three hundred sixty an hour. "It's dust," he said. "Just imagine: six-billion-year-old dust burning like that." An incoming fireball dropped in hard and exploded over our heads, and we yelped—in fear or wonder, I don't know. It was cold and the edge of my bag was frosting up. Still the stars fell all around us. They fell and fell; every time I opened my eyes, they were falling.

I woke up in a silver haze. Clouds ringed the mountainsides. As tundra swans whooped on the lake, a skein of geese slowly untangled over our heads. The soil was a cathedral of crystals growing upward, pushing little roofs of dirt. Brilliant hoarfrost covered the entire world, sparkling on our sleeping bags, our hats, each branch of every tree, every bent reed. It was as if all those twinkling white stars that fell out of the sky, all that bright six-billion-year-old interstellar dust had fallen glittering on the branches while we were sleeping, dusted our hats, drifted into the folds of our blankets. Fallen stars stuck to spiderwebs and outlined every blade of grass.

Sometimes I think I see a miracle, and then I realize that it's just the everyday working of the world. Warm moist air encounters cold air and turns to shards of ice.

Light catches the crystal planes. Tundra swans fly in to feed. Geese cry out. The lake reflects the sky. That's the real miracle: that it's no miracle at all, just Earth, sailing on in the dark.

SONGS IN THE NIGHT

WE HAD COME LATE to the coastal dunes, back-packing in by the unreliable light of headlamps. It's a challenge, pitching a tent in the dark, throwing sabers of light everywhere you look, knowing that if you put down a tent pole or a stake, it will be lost until moonrise or morning. But we got the tent up and then sat on our packs in front of the door, listening to the night.

When Frank finally crawls into a tent, he falls asleep like a bag of sand dropping off a truck. I think the whole point of sleeping out is to stay awake as long as I can, listening. I bragged to Frank that he could lead me any-where blindfolded, or with a pillowcase over my head, and I would know by the sounds what time it was, and where he had pitched the tent. He pointed out that he usually knows where he is, and it doesn't matter what time it is, if he is happily asleep. But I know he wakes up in the night and listens, and he wonders what makes the sounds—not what animal is calling, but by what physical process the sound comes to be.

The wind sifted dry reeds in front of the tent, tiny claws scrabbled against rough bark behind it. Tree frogs clattered from all directions. A killdeer called. Surf rumbled like a thunderstorm on a far horizon, and close at hand, water slipped softly in and out over sand, like the breath of a person who is not afraid. So I inferred that it was late, maybe midnight, on a freshwater lake behind the foredune on the Oregon coast, on sand between shore pines and a tule marsh. "Good guess," Frank said, looking out over the marsh in the moonlight, and the dunes beyond.

I'm not especially good at recognizing birds by their calls, but I do know the killdeer. It calls its name in the night, not exactly *killdeer,* but more like *tewdew, tewdew,* over and over. Last summer, when I was teaching at an island camp, I met a man who could do a perfect imitation of a killdeer. He was a fish physiologist, a quiet man who struggled to put thoughts into words—but damn, he could do birds. His meadowlark was exactly right, even with that little roll of water at the end, the lick of a stream lifting over a rock. He could do a mouse well enough to turn a kestrel's head—I saw it happen—and his loon, my god, a loon to bring tears to your eyes, the long sad call. I watched him work with cedar waxwings in a clearing on the island, practicing the slip, the tight little whistle, until the waxwings were giving it back to him, correcting him gently, and he answered them until he had it right.

When he was a little kid, he told me, he had to get up early for his paper route. Every morning, he was alone in the dim, empty street, except for mourning doves, calling. He started to answer them, he said, and before long, the doves began to follow him—a lonely little kid weaving down the street on his bicycle, balancing a canvas bag of newspapers, trailing mourning doves, and cooing.

He turns away from people when he whistles, so no one ever sees him make the sound. He has to twist his face to get it right, he explained, and he's self-conscious about the shape his mouth takes on. One evening, I saw him standing alone at the end of the dock as the last of the color left the sky. I heard a loon calling, so I scanned the empty horizon with binoculars, then turned to study the broad back and averted head of a man who was crying out as if his heart would break.

At the breakfast table the next morning, I was leafing through bird books, trying to identify the owl that had called in the birches all night. "Was it like this?" the man asked, and out came a rough hooing with a gulp at the end, and that was it, exactly. "So it's the barred owl," he said, "who gives us songs in the night."

"Who gives us songs in the night." I recognized the phrase from Job and thought how strange it was that a fish biologist would talk that way. Back in my office, I looked the passage up. Job 35:10. Job has been complaining to Elihu about his misfortunes—and who can blame him, having suffered, after all, the trials of Job? But Elihu says, people call for help from God, but no one praises God the Maker, who gives us songs in the night. That's the one gift Elihu wanted Job to take account of especially—the songs.

I have to say, the Bible never fails to confound me. But I wanted to know what *songs* meant to Job, so I carried the text down the hall to my colleague, who found the passage in his copy of the Parallel Bible, a book that sets translations side by side. It turns out that *songs* is translated differently in every edition of the Bible.

In the New Jerusalem Bible, it's "Who makes *glad songs* at night." And I thought, yes, this translator would understand what it's like to sleep on a beach with the frogs in full chorus and the coots hooting like drunks. The glad songs.

And in the New Revised Standard Version it's "Who gives us *strength* in the night." And I thought, this is a translator who has come onto the dunes on a night when the wind lifted sand and sent it streaming like the Milky Way over the escarpment where a mountain lion stood, watching the dunes, white under the moon.

And the Revised English Bible says, "Who gives us *protection* by night." I thought, this translator must have slept on an island in bear country, right on the soft sweet ground, right there in the salmonberries and sword ferns. He has known, from the trilling of spring peepers and the hoot of a great horned owl, that all is well. All is well: there are no bears afoot on this dark night.

But the New American Bible says, "Who gives us *vision* in the night." And I wondered, did this translator know the sudden seeing that has nothing to do with eyes?—that clear, sharp knowing that comes only once or twice in a lifetime, the grateful understanding, like waking up from a dream of a dark street to find the sun in your eyes and nuthatches fussing in the ponderosa pines, and never has light been so luminous or colors so clear.

I wish I knew that one Hebrew word that means *vision* and *strength* and *protection* and *glad songs*. This is a word I could use. This is a word teachers should drill in fifth-grade vocabulary lessons, the language of praise and celebration, a word I should teach to the man who sings like a cedar waxwing.

FRANK AND I HAD STAYED up late in camp, brewing tea and talking. Bats stayed out late, too, zinging past our heads. Frank's guess was the little brown myotis, but it's hard to know. They were just dark motes veering around, fluttering their wings so fast they disappeared. A hunting bat sprays out a constant stream of high pulsing squeaks beyond the limit of human hearing. When a sound wave hits an insect, it bounces a signal back to the bat, who swoops in and catches the insect in its net—its tail spread between its legs like an apron. Once we were sitting beside a river in the evening, maybe the Deschutes or the Rogue—it was a long time ago. Suddenly moths let their wings go limp and flopped spastically to the stones. Frank said a bat must be hunting; the moths felt the sound pepper their wings and took evasive action.

I asked Frank how bats keep up that constant barrage of sound. I can't imagine dropping from the ceiling of a cave, flapping my wings so fast I fly like the wind, and while I'm doing this, sending out an unending fusillade of squeaks. I could fly or squeak probably, but not both at the same time. The energetics are tough here, he said. As it turns out, bats' wings work like bellows. Every time a bat forces its wings down, the muscles compress its chest and send a puff of air through the reeds in its throat. A bat works on the same principle as the organist who pumps away at the foot pedals on the organ, until the organ exhales Bach.

We were surprised how long it took before the frogs started to sing. The music always starts with one. Then frog after frog starts sawing away. The chorus finally started in the marsh past our feet and spread up the shoreline like a wave at a basketball game, until we were awash in frog song. It's a mystery to me, how small a tree frog is and how big its song. I tried to picture a singing frog. I imagined blowing up a balloon—the pressure in my ears, the squeeze of my diaphragm. I imagined blowing up a balloon made of my own neck skin. I blow it up until I am twice my size. Now I hold the air in and tremble. Imagine: it's hard enough for a human to make a sound that carries a mile, but imagine holding that note all night long. Now imagine this feat from a frog the size of a thumb.

The energetics of this music are formidable, too—so much energy expended, it could kill a frog. Some tree frogs have only enough energy to sing for three nights, scientists have learned. That is how long they have: three trembling nights to sing a song so glad, so strong that a female heavy with eggs frog-strokes through threads of algae, risking largemouth bass, risking great blue herons, unable to stay away from that song. Now when I hear a frog chorus, I think of the silence of the frogs on day four.

Our ancestors made themselves silent and small when they found themselves alone in the night. If they dreamed, they dreamed without a sound. I know I can't scream in a dream; I don't know if anyone can. Chased by dark forms darting through circles of light under streetlamps, I push air toward my lips, but it's as if they were sewn shut with black threads. All that comes out is a muffled cry from the back of my throat. And of course it has to be this way. If our ancestors cried out in the night, predators for half a mile around would prick up their ears and slowly turn their heads toward the source of the sound. At night, humans listen, and this is wise.

We sat quietly for a long time, listening to the frogs. Ground fog, which had been quietly rising from the marsh, began to reach toward us with ragged fingers. Clouds were suddenly on the move, breaking into an armada of small ships slowly sailing past the moon. We could go into our sleeping bags or freeze, so we went to bed, leaving the tent open to the sounds.

SHOREBIRDS BEGAN TO CALL at first light, their voices high, piercing, and sharp. I pulled warm piles of sleeping bag to my chin and lay there listening, glad to be awake again on such a morning. Spotted sandpipers hurried over broken reeds, peeping endlessly. The clouds were low on the dunes, but there was no sign of rain. A Caspian tern sailed across the lily pads, screeching with a voice so sharp and tough, I felt it could scrape off the top of my head. The calls of shorebirds, which evolved at the edge of the sea, have a high frequency, audible over the low rumble of surf. In the forest, birds have low-frequency voices, because the long wavelengths of the low tones are not as quickly scattered or absorbed by the tangle of leaves and moss. I've read that birds on the floor of a jungle sing in lower voices than birds in the tops of the same trees, and the northern forests carry the basso profundo voices of the owls and the grouse.

But put a bird in an open meadow or marshland where sound can carry forever in the sunlit silence: here are the voices so beautiful to the human, also a savanna creature. As the sun brightened the sky behind the forest, I heard a meadowlark's slippery warble, as joyous a birdsong as there ever was, *sleep loo lidi lidijuvi* across a marshy swale, and, when the new sun flared under the clouds, the red-winged blackbird. The red-wing's call is a celebration, *okalee-ah*, and a soft *schlick, schlick,* like a knife slicing water.

A week or so ago, I was talking to a young couple from Turkey. They were very polite, but it was clear they were fed up with the English language. Turkish, they said, had just enough words. A word for everything, but not a lot of extra words. English on the other hand: they gestured extravagantly with their hands to show me how big the dictionary is. Too many words, wasted.

Well, yes. I could get along with *automobile* and forget all the synonyms. *Telephone* is adequate for all my purposes. But English has a dangerous shortage of words for the feeling you get when you hear sandpipers in the morning, that mix of safe and glad and healthy and seeing right into the center of things (even now, I fumble for words). English used to have good words, but they have been stolen and wrecked or perverted. We need to invent new words, or march down the street and wrest back the words that have been taken from us—or find exactly the right word in Turkish and borrow that. It will not do to find ourselves suddenly mute, or inexact, or misunderstood, when we need to tell someone how this beautiful world speaks to us.

I want to take back *amazing*. People say, did you see that amazing slam dunk? But amazing should mean what it says: caught in a maze, confused by many ways, not knowing where to go. To be a-mazed is to be be-wildered. Amazing is half wonder and half terror, trapped among branching paths in a wilderness of wind-tangled beach pine and tentacled rhododendrons in bloom. A hiker is amazed when, finding herself lost with night coming on, she sits down to think harder than she ever has in her life, all her senses blazing and her mind on fire.

And *astonishment*. This world needs *astonishment*. It comes from the Latin word *tonus*, which means thunder. To be astonished is to be thunderstruck, knocked backward by a sudden blow. This is how Shakespeare's

character can say, "Captain, you have astonished him,"
as the victim lies stunned on the stage. Outside of the
Arctic, where I'm told there is no lightning, I would
guess that everyone has been literally astonished. You
see something so blindingly bright, so surprising that
you close your eyes and brace yourself physically for the
blow that comes next, the thunderous crack. I think an
osprey must be astonished each time it crashes through
the wall between sky and water, and maybe that's what
astonishment is, this sudden entrance into another world.

Awesome. Awe means intense fear or dread, from the
same roots as ail, trouble, affliction, and wound. Have
you ever heard something so beautiful that you were
filled with fear? *Where were you when the morning stars
sang together, and all the sons of God shouted for joy?* And
Job answered, *I lay my hand on my mouth. I repent in dust
and ashes.* People sometimes say things like "awesome
haircut." But people shouldn't mess with awe.

And shall we try to reclaim *holy* from the saints? That
word used to make me angry. I'd be reading along in
some nature writer, and I'd bump up against the word
holy, and I had no idea what it meant and I was suspicious that the writer didn't either. It was a placeholder, a
stuntman doing the dangerous work, representing something, but who knows what? All the same, I've come to
believe that we need to find some way to talk about the
secular holy. *Holy* comes from the word for whole, and
whole means healthy, unhurt, complete, entire. In the
midst of all the fragmented ecosystems, all the broken up,

stripped down, hacked up, reamed out places, there are places that are still whole, places that speak to our whole selves, entire. Scientists call them intact ecosystems. Aldo Leopold referred to them as having integrity. Does it hurt to call them holy?

Which brings us to *love*. I once spoke to a convention of National Park Rangers, people who love the land if anybody does—intently, pragmatically, in the rhythm of their daily lives. "I like what you say," one ranger commented afterward, "but I wonder if you couldn't say it without using the L-word." I didn't now how to answer. It isn't enough to point out that Hallmark has kidnapped the word *love* and beaten it senseless. My first instinct was to think that the ranger shared in the sadness of all science, its loneliness—generations of scientists and land managers thrilled by natural creation, but trained, like secret lovers, to a deep and steady silence about their feelings toward what they study so intently.

Physicist and essayist Chet Raymo thinks that one of the results of the split between spiritual and scientific views of the world is that science has lost the ability to celebrate natural creation. "In going their separate ways," Raymo wrote, "the Church and science were each impoverished . . . and science was deprived of access to the Church's rich traditional language of praise." And more, he implies: to the extent that science has become the dominant western worldview, we have all lost the language of praise.

But I'm not so sure. I had asked the park ranger, "So what word shall we use instead of l--e?"

He thought for a long time before he answered. "Maybe, instead, we should say *listen to*."

Listen to. To hear with thoughtful attention.

To hold something in your hand, to attend to it, to be astonished by it, to devote your life to its mysteries, to name it precisely, to go deeper and deeper into how it comes to be, to truly pay attention to it, to honor it by listening closely—isn't this what scientists do each day? There's more than one way to love the world.

"DID YOU KNOW," Frank asked me, "that some owls have uneven ears?"

He had wakened me to listen to a barn owl across the lake. This happens all the time: I think I'm awake and he's asleep, but he has to wake me up to hear the songs.

If you're going to find something in the dark, he explained carefully, one sort of ear isn't good enough. Symmetrical ears will tell you where the prey is on a horizontal plane, if the ears are far enough apart. If a mouse is squeaking straight in front of you, the sound will be the same in both ears; but if it's off to the side, the sound will come first to the closest ear, and with a different volume and tone. Then you can swivel your head like a radar dish until you're looking straight at that invisible mouse. But how will you know if it's above or below that plane? For this, owls need asymmetrical ears. The ear hole is higher on one side than on the other. When the squeaking is equally loud in both ears, the mouse is at ear level. With its widespread, uneven ears, an owl can put a mouse right in the crosshairs of its hearing. *Binaural localization:* that's the language the scientists use, the precise words for this particular species of marvel.

Across the lake, air passed through the owl's syrinx, a bony structure at the bottom of the trachea. Specialized muscles tightened and loosened the membranes in the syrinx, tuning it like the skin of a drum. Another owl answered from the forest. Surf rumbled behind the hill of sand. A train whistle blew far away, as if someone were pressing his whole palm on the keys of an organ. Frank and I listened with our odd, uneven ears. *Lift up your heads, and be lifted up. Sing praises.*

THE INHERITANCE
OF ACQUIRED
CHARACTERISTICS

THE MOVING MEN HAVE COME and gone, so now I
have my father's desk. Forty years ago, the desk took up
one side of the room that served as both a study for my
father and a bedroom I shared with my sisters. Triple
bunks filled the opposite side of the room, three little
girls stacked on shelves in perfect symmetry to the book-
shelves stacked above the desk. But now the desk is sitting in the middle of my study, empty drawers hanging
open.

It's a beautiful piece of mahogany furniture but an
awkward fit to my work—made for a fountain pen, not
a computer. Even the shape is old-fashioned; it must
have been designed for a writer who could sit still, with
her knees stuck in the kneehole. All my stuff slouches in
piles on the floor, ready to be rearranged in his drawers.
I remember where everything is supposed to go—typing
paper in the lower left-hand drawer, hole punch on the
chalked outline of a hole punch, his thesaurus in reach

of his right hand, and in the top drawer, a model of the double helix made from drinking straws.

But I've inherited so many memories along with this desk, I'm not sure if there's room inside for anything else. The wooden knock of the opening drawer, the smell of pencil lead and mimeographed tests, and here is my father, working under a draftsman's lamp while we three fall asleep listening to his pen rustle on paper.

MY SISTERS AND I crowd around my father's desk, rummaging in the top left drawer for scissors. Carefully, we cut shapes from black tape—a flower, maybe, a tree or a bird. We carry the shapes to the backyard and stick them to green apples hanging on the tree. As the summer warms to autumn, the apples turn red, but only where the sun hits them. When the time comes to pick those apples, we peel off the tape, and there are red apples decorated with soaring green birds and tiger lilies. We cut the apples with great ceremony, and eat the birds last.

WITH THE POCKETKNIFE he keeps in the top middle drawer, my father cuts a slit diagonally into the bark of a twig on the apple tree. He cuts a twig from a different apple tree, wedges it into the slit, covers the whole junction with some goo like Vaseline, and binds it tight with strips of rubber from old bicycle tires. In winter, when cardinals shake snow from the branches, chickadees and nuthatches fill the tree with movement, pecking upside down at the graft, opening the wounds for insects. But come spring, the apple tree blooms with pink flowers—and here and there a spray of white flowers, or dark pink, almost purple. In autumn, most of the tree's apples are red, but some are yellow, and some grow like bunches of cherries, small and dark.

MY SISTERS AND I tag along with my father to Baldwin-Wallace College, where he teaches. While he works in a classroom, we wander into the greenhouse, which smells good and green, like stones from the bottom of a river. Then we go into the bird room where there are long counters full of wooden drawers. Each contains a dead bird. I pull open a drawer, and here is a redheaded woodpecker, hard and stiff. It's lying on its back, which is somehow one straight line from the tip of its beak to the end of its bristly tail. Its legs are bent into the air, and its black toes are curled tight. My father wants us to notice its beak, so hard, and we grasp the woodpecker and peck the back of our hands experimentally, but all we really notice is how dead it is and unlike anything that might once have flown.

IN THE BACKYARD of our house, my father is growing polka-dotted eggplants. This is Ohio, with Ohio summers, steamy and hot and prickly with mosquitoes—good eggplant weather. When the fruits are the size of fists, my father takes a metal tube and cuts round holes in each eggplant, carefully saving the cores. Then he sticks purple cores in the holes in the white eggplants, and white cores in the purple eggplants, creating spotted eggplants as cheerful as Easter eggs. The eggplants grow well enough this way and set seed, which my father carefully collects and keeps in labeled envelopes in the middle right-hand drawer of his desk. The next spring, he plants the seeds and waits half the summer to see if his eggplants grow spots. Of course, the next generation is as solid shiny purple or as consistently white as any old eggplants would ever be.

My father is delighted. He waltzes around the backyard with plain-Jane eggplants in each hand. This is the Cold War, carried on right here in our backyard, and the eggplants are my father's contribution to the war effort. T. D. Lysenko, Stalin's chief scientist, insists that plants and animals can pass on to their offspring characteristics they acquire during their lifetimes. Teach a dog to fear a beating, Lysenkoists say, and it will bear little cringing pups; graft black fur onto a white hamster, and you will have baby hamsters as spotted as Holstein cows. The inheritance of acquired characteristics? My father doesn't believe it for a minute. But he grows evidence against the theory, year after year, even when not one of us will eat the polka-dotted eggplants or allow a single piece to touch her fork.

AND NOW HERE I AM, sitting at this desk, having inherited all those Ohio summers and the dusty dove-tailed drawers spotted with India ink. I don't believe

Lysenko either. But I know that people carry something of their childhoods in them, and sometimes they pass that on to their children in turn. It's a mystery, the legacy a parent leaves a child—the encoded DNA; the hard, dead memories and the ones that take flight; the hopes and astonishments grafted to wounds where birds still gather; all the things we make ourselves from. But the next generation is the test, and the mystery that's on my mind as my children grow up and move away is what part of their grandfather they will take with them as they go.

My father taught genetics; he studied all this. He taught students about the double helix the very year it was discovered. So I wish he were here to explain why the smell of apple blossoms startles me, like a tap on the shoulder when there's no one there. I want to know *how it is exactly* that the father is roots to his daughter's branches, and how he lives in the daughter—not just in her memories, but in the fruit she bears. And then, I wish he could stand by me in the airport as my children disappear down carpeted hallways and make me believe that the gifts he so deliberately passed on to his children will live in his grandchildren as well.

Fact is, I never asked him how to raise a child; I didn't think of him as that kind of expert, and we lived so far apart. But I remember bringing Erin to visit when she was just learning to crawl. It was a nice autumn afternoon, so we went out to the backyard under that apple tree—no decorator apples that year, but a mirror rigged over a dove's nest, where my father spied on the babies as they fledged. I spread a baby blanket and put Erin right in the center with a rattle and her fuzzy eagle. She kept crawling toward the edge, and I kept putting her back in the middle. Finally, my father picked her up and set her down in the grass. Then he gave the blanket a quick flip, scattering the rattle and the eagle, and folded it up and set it aside.

But after this, my memories of our children leave home and hit the road. We had moved to the West Coast. Except for Christmas and maybe a week in the summer, I have no memories of my parents with my children. We never gave our children a desk to gather around; I guess instead we gave them the edge of water.

❦

WITH OUR TINY DAUGHTER, Frank and I are camped on the North Platte River in Wyoming, a day late in September when aspens blink in light reflected off moving water and cottonwood leaves crackle under our feet. Erin is five months old. All day long, I walk along the river, carrying Erin inside my coat. At night, Frank and I sit cross-legged in the tent, looking out the open door. The baby is asleep in Frank's arms. Snowflakes fall softly down, and aspen leaves drift off the branches and float onto a field of snow.

❦

NOW I HAVE ERIN by the straps of her overalls, trying to keep her from falling over the bank of a creek in the Oregon dunes. Frank has Jonathan in a backpack under

a bright umbrella tied to the pack frame. With his pants
rolled up to his knees, Frank wades down the center of
the creek. Jonathan jumps up and down in the pack, trying to reach the water, and the umbrella flutters with the
jumping, snapping off sprays of coastal rain.

PILED INTO A DUSTY CAR, we're driving across
Coffeepot Flat on tracks more and more deeply rutted,
down through a gate in a barbwire fence, through a herd
of range cattle, through a cut in the bluff, to deep grass
along the river. With water in sight, the children are
finally, blessedly, quiet. When we pull to a stop, I look in
the backseat and there they are, bug-eyed in diving masks
and fins, with black rubber snorkels shoved behind their
lips. They slide out of the car and flap across the grass.
Soon we hear voices bubbling thick and joyous from the
tops of snorkels. We can't understand a word they say.

IT'S DEEP DUSK AT the landing. The Rogue River is
rushing by like a fleet of trucks. My husband and children are three hours overdue from a float trip. That they
are in trouble I know for sure; what kind of trouble, I can
only imagine. I will walk on stones, step-by-step, until
I get to one hundred. Then I will reverse direction and
walk on another hundred stones. Six hundred and forty
stones, and my young son appears on the beach. I fold

him in my arms. "Jonny, where are the others?" But here they come, soaking wet and shaking. The current had pinned their boat against a rock. Then the boat turned turtle and spun away, leaving them stranded on an island.

☙

I'M STANDING ON a bridge over the Charles River with the other parents. The river makes a sharp bend just downstream, so we can't see the boats coming, but we can hear the coxswains shouting in the distance. Now here come the boats and I sweep the river with binoculars, trying to see my daughter. I can make out the yellow shirts, so this must be her team, but it's only when the shell is directly underneath that I think I recognize Erin, and even then, I'm guessing from her position in the boat. When this race is over, the young women will carry the boats on their shoulders, a beautiful pageantry of color, oars raised high like banners, and I will hug Erin good-bye and leave to catch my flight back to Oregon.

☙

WE HAVE A POSTCARD from Jonathan, with his college biology class in Australia for all of winter term. "We're on Heron Island, out in the Great Barrier Reef. This place is awesome. I was sleeping on the beach last night, when I felt something tickling my face. I held as still as I could, because baby sea turtles were crawling over my face, my chest, my legs—tiny little turtle feet, walking to the ocean. I think this is the happiest I have ever been in my life. Love you. Wish you were here."

ALL THESE STORIES REMIND me of one spring Sunday, when my father drove me and my sisters to a silted pond and filled a big glass jar with water. We brought the jar back to his desk and watched the life emerge as the silt settled—brilliant red water mites, daphne and fairy shrimp, back-striders and dragonfly nymphs, and best of all, the larval stages of caddis flies, walking around with only their heads and front legs sticking out of tubes they'd made from flecks of sand and tiny sticks.

With tweezers, my father gently pulled the tube off a caddis larva so we could see it build a new case from detritus in the jar. Entering into the spirit of the experiment, my sisters and I decided that sticks and sand were not good enough for our larva; we would give it the most extravagantly glamorous building materials we could find. Into the jar went shreds of birthday ribbon, gold and silver glitter, glass beads, and tinsel.

All night, our larva lay naked in the glitz—a long-bodied, bandy-legged black insect. Then, early the next morning, it spun a silk thread, winding it around and around its body, guiding the strands carefully with delicate legs. When it was fully encased in a sticky tube of threads, it groped over the glass, feeling its way, touching everything. It picked up a shred of silver ribbon and stuck it to its tube. We cheered and pressed our faces closer to the glass. It stuck on a blue bead. Stumbling into the pile of glitter, it pressed a flake to the opening of the case.

But the larva was moving more and more slowly, touching fewer and fewer things, and then, seeming to be disheartened, it stopped building entirely and slumped on the bottom of the jar. This scared us. We had expected a glorious creation. But the larva's tube was pathetic—discarded ribbon stuck at an odd angle, a bead like a wart. We took the jar back to the river, dumped the whole mess, and watched as glitter settled into the silt.

Now that Frank and I are parents with grown children of our own, I don't know any more than I ever did about what makes children who they are, what wild mix of memory and genetic destiny and the everyday furniture of a life—river sand, a father's hand, the angle of the sun. But I suspect that parents don't make their children: like the pond to the caddis fly larvae, we give the materials to our children and they make themselves, memory by memory. So the question for any parent is, what do we want our children to be made of? And as they grow up and away, so far from home, what do we want them to take with them, what sources of strength and delight?

THE ROAD TO CAPE PERPETUA

IT TAKES A STRONG STOMACH to drive over the
Coast Range from my house to the Pacific Ocean. The
road goes the way of the rivers, following tight curves
between the hills. Logging trucks crowd the turns,
going the other way. They downshift to hold heavy loads
against the grade. Over the crest of the range, in the
green tumble of hills that form the headwaters for the
coastal salmon streams, each curve uncovers another
square of bare mountainside, clear-cut to the mud.
There's hardly a green leaf left in the cut—only gray dirt,
shattered tree trunks lying every which way, and root
wads and dead branches bulldozed into muddy piles.
Even the rivers are gray, muddied by rain that erodes
the raw draglines.

I drove as fast as I could through this part, keeping my eyes on the single row of alders that the logging company left along the road to hide the carnage.
I knew that on the coast, just south of Cape Perpetua,

I would come finally to remnant patches of ancient rain forest, somehow saved from the crosscut saws — six-hundred-year-old Sitka spruce and red cedars that grow, dark and mossy, down the slope to the edge of the sea. I pushed through the scarred hills, trying to concentrate on how the ancient forest would smell — all damp earth and cedar — and how surf sounds, far away through deep ferns.

SOUTH OF THE CAPE, I walked a trail under Sitka spruce to the edge of a cliff, where the forest cracks off into the sea. On the headland, the air was suddenly salt-thick and cold, the wind ferocious. In wild surf, scuds of sea foam sprang up like startled birds, and wave-tossed logs shot ten feet in the air. A few children ran shouting along the cliff edge, holding their hats against the gale, ducking under sheets of spray, changing course simultaneously, like sanderlings. I pulled my windbreaker tight around me and sat on a bench overlooking the sea.

The bench was a memorial. Someone who deeply loves the coast must have chosen the site, just above the wild collision of coastal stream and cobbles. I read the inscription on the brass plaque: *Mother, When you hear a song or see a bird, please do not let the thought of me be sad, for I am loving you just as I always have. It was heaven here with you.*

A living, grieving mother must have written this note, as if her child were not dead, but was speaking to her through the sea of her pain. And the heaven they shared?

It must have been here, in this exact spot, where the sea surges into the river at high tide, and gulls stand hip-deep, shouldering fresh water across their backs, as they must have done for centuries.

I imagined a mother pulling rainpants on a child already dancing to go. A last pat on his wool hat, and he runs across the grass in too-big boots. She pulls on her own raincoat and follows him down the trail. At the cliff edge, she stands beside him in the wind, looking out to sea.

How can she live with the sorrow?

We're told by psychologist Elisabeth Kübler-Ross that there is a pattern to grief: everyone must make the same terrible journey, putting one foot in front of the other in air suddenly gone cold and thick. My friend Katherine, who knows many kinds of sorrow, agrees with Kübler-Ross, and wonders if people who are mourning the loss of a beloved part of the world—a forest, a salmon run, a species, a stream—don't experience some of the same feelings as those who mourn the loss of a human being. The quality of the pain may be different, and its intensity, she says, but the sequence of steps is familiar.

Denial is often the first reaction to loss, Kübler-Ross says. Maybe the forest isn't really dead. All those seeds hiding in the bulldozed ground—they might grow into a forest eventually. And if it's too late to save this forest, isn't there still time to save the forests on the other side of the mountains? And maybe the salmon runs aren't extinct; the salmon might be waiting in the ocean until the rivers clear and silt washes off the spawning beds.

"Look around," my neighbor says, trying to lift my spirits. "It's still a beautiful world. The environmental crisis is just a protest-industry fund-raising scam."

The next stage is anger. What kind of person can cut an ancient forest to bloody stumps, bulldoze the meadows to mud, spray poison over the mess that's left, and then set smudge fires in the slash? And when the wounded mountainside slumps into the river, floods tear apart the waterfalls and scour the spawning beds, and no salmon return, what kind of person can pronounce it an act of God—and then direct the bulldozers through the stream and into the next forest, and the next? I hope there's a cave in hell for people like this, where an insane little demon hops around shouting, "jobs or trees, jobs or trees," and buries an ax blade in their knees every time they struggle to their feet.

Step three. Bargaining. Look, we're rational people. Let's work this out. Destroy this forest if you have to, but plant new seedlings in the slash. Drain this wetland and build your stupid Wal-Mart, but dig a new swamp next to the highway. Let cattle trample this riverbank and plop in this headwater, but fence them from this spawning bed. Kill the smolts in your turbines, but buy new fish for another stream. Then let's create community and study the issue again in five years.

Step four. Depression. Hopelessness deep and dark enough to drown in.

And gradually, disastrously, grief's final step: acceptance.

On the Oregon coast, the children know mostly

fish-poor, flood-stripped streams. Here, all estuaries are fouled, and no river water is safe to drink. That's the way it is. Why should they think it could be any different? Children who have never seen an ancient forest climb the huge, crumbling, blood-red stumps as they might climb onto the lap of a vacant-faced grandfather. They look out over the ferns and hemlock seedlings, unable to imagine what used to be. They don't remember waking up to birdsong. How can they miss a murrelet if they've never seen one? It's not just their landscape that has been clear-cut, but their imaginations, the wide expanse of their hope.

And when their grandparents' memories of unbroken forests fade, and the old stories get tedious—the streams of red salmon pushing into the river—and the photograph albums hold dry images of some other place, some other time, then another opening in the universe slams shut, another set of possibilities disappears forever.

Ecologists call this the sliding baseline; what we accept as normal is gradually changing. This is what we must resist: finally coming to accept that a stripped down, dammed up, paved over, poisoned, bulldozed, radioactive, impoverished landscape is the norm—the way it's supposed to be, the way it's always been, the way it must always be. This is the result we should fear the most.

❦

I TURNED AWAY FROM the ocean and hiked back into the forest. It was dark there, and noisy with wind and distant surf. Shadows sank into the whorls of maiden-hair ferns and shaggy trunks of cedars centuries old. The decaying earth was a black granite wall bearing the names of all that had been lost and forgotten on the far side of the mountain: the footprints of cougar and elk, yellow-bellied salamanders pacing across dark duff, sword ferns unfurling, the flute of the varied thrush, the smell of cedar and soil; the wild coastal river, its headwaters buried in mossy logs, its waters leaping with salmon, its beaches dangerous with surf and swaying bears. Kneeling, I traced a heron's tracks engraved in black soil at the edge of the stream.

Into the shadows, light fell like soft rain. It shone on every hemlock needle and huckleberry, each lifted leaf of sorrel. A winter wren sang somewhere in the salal, and a raven called from far away. I leaned against an ancient Douglas-fir that soared to great height and disappeared into the overcast.

The wilderness is a witness, standing tall and terrible in the storm at the edge of the sea. A wild forest confronts us with what we have done. It reminds us of what we have lost. And it gives us a vision of what—in some way—might live again.

THIS WILL NOT COME AGAIN

ON COASTAL RIVERS in autumn, when light is low and yellow and the river pools above the riffles, water shines slick as obsidian. Floating vine maple leaves dent the river, as if their flaming colors were hot enough to melt black glass. Between the Pacific and the riffles many miles upstream, the river stretches out in tidewater, rising and sinking twice each day, lifting the ferns and laying them down again, gathering alder leaves from the gravel bars and floating them in slow circles on the eddies.

Frank and I launched in late afternoon on a slack high tide. As we rowed away upstream, the drift boat floated on a reflection of a drift boat floating on the sky, the long oars pulling against their own images. Each pull of the oars rippled the sky and lifted the smell of water. I leaned over the bow to watch for the salmon that have always surged into the river in October, but all I could see was the reflection of my own face, awash in the bow wave.

In the riverbed, the air turned cold. A mile. Another, and we pulled on our jackets. Color faded out of the landscape, the red vine maples darkening first, the yellow alders the last to go. Along the length of a willow thicket, we followed a wedge of light that must have been a beaver. The lines veered toward the bank and disappeared. As we rowed the last mile, a string of mergansers beat upriver to some nighttime roost. Finally, at nightfall, we slid into a still pool above an island and dropped anchor.

Pulling a knife from his pocket, Frank whittled the stub end of a candle and wedged it into the mouth of a beer can propped in the bow. By the small, wavering light, we perched on either gunwale, drinking tea from a thermos, and listened to the last of the robins. Then we spread our sleeping bags and lay on the floor of the boat in the dark, only a layer of goose down and the wooden hull between the river and our cheeks.

We weren't afraid, swinging from the anchor line in deep pools of darkness, and we weren't tired, but curious and excited, like little children who are seldom out so late. Dusk is a borderland. The boundary between day and night bounces images off its shiny black surface. To see into the night, you have to wade into darkness, let it rise to your waist, your shoulders, over your head, until you lift and float, swaying, and night washes into your mind and presses against your chest.

At night, the boundaries of our bodies fade into darkness, and we become pure feeling extended into space. The substance of the world fades, too, leaving only sense impressions—the sweetness of the trees, the dampness of the air. Lying in the boat, I am perception and speculation linked by moving air to the universe. A cedar dissolves into scent and washes into my mind. A deer's snort hangs, disembodied, above the river, and then the river disappears, leaving only its smells and sound.

The tide passed under us, lowering us close to the gravel bed. When we woke near midnight, we heard the sound of bubbles touching against the boat, a musical sound, like children playing far away. As the tide rose again, it lifted us with a sensation not of rising but of hushing, then, toward high tide, of silence, the perfect silence of pooled water. The boat swung on the anchor rope and stars circled to the north, to the south, to the north, as if time had lost its sense of direction.

We listened for the splash of salmon breaching and falling heavily on their sides—but none came. There should have been salmon leaping all around us, smashing back into the water, as if a crowd had gathered to heave logs into the river. I rolled over to listen more closely, rocking the boat. The movement of the boat faded to dew-muffled silence and the *tap tap* of moisture dripping from the trees.

Smells moved in gradually: in still air, the smell of damp ferns relaxing, settling against the sand, releasing the vapors of the mud at their roots, the nests of willow leaves caught in their stems. When air moved softly downriver, the smells of river water seeped into the boat, autumn leaves and the roots of hemlocks. And when warm air rising from the hills pulled sea fret up the riverbed, I smelled salt and motor oil and the breath of fish, and iridescent piles of kelp torn from the sea and half buried in sand.

Sometime after midnight, we awoke to find sea fog rising in white flames behind the forest, silhouetting the branches of alder and fir. The fog bank grew slowly until all the sky was suffused with white light. When Frank turned on his flashlight, we discovered that we were caught in a miniature gale; in the beam of light, droplets swirled in little tempests, gusting and blowing sprays of dew, shooting skyward, then falling, then caught again and carried up by tiny tornado winds. Frank switched off the light, the storm disappeared, and all I could feel was moisture on my face, all I could see was the milky sky. I closed my eyes and the drift boat softened beneath me, moving as I moved, breathing as I breathed, quietly, slowly, cool and damp.

🐝

EARLY MORNING. Fog filled the river bank to bank. Standing in the drift boat, Frank rowed toward the island. The hull ground against gravel and I climbed out to start a breakfast fire on the beach. When he rowed out again, all I could see above the fog was the silhouette of Frank's head and shoulders, the fly line, curling, and the sharp bow of the boat. I stood on the beach, listening intently for a jack salmon to slap as it unfolded after a fly.

Following deer tracks through sand and ferns, I climbed the bank of the island into the light. Sunlight created a new world here, bringing the kinglets to life and making a hidden deer sneeze. Stumps rose through the third-growth alder. The cutover land had grown back to nettles and blackberries, but the forest might as well have been made of spiderwebs, an infinitude of spider-webs in the shape of fir trees and wild roses, gracing the air like light come to life.

Everything on the island was cold and wet—the stones, the sticks, the hard-boiled eggs, the wrinkled alder leaves—but I had brought matches and candle stubs and cedar staves from home. Soon steam from the teapot sank into the wood smoke that sank into the fog that floated on the river. Near the island, the world was perfectly double, the arc of an alder limb echoed in another arc below it, and when a leaf dropped to the water, another floated out of the depths to meet it. A reflection of crows flapped upside down in the river, their wingtips reaching toward cawing counterparts in the sky.

Light grew behind the alders, as if the forest floor were on fire, and then sunlight striped the stones. I stood in the warmth of a stripe, holding a mug of tea against my chest, squinting in the steam. The fog sorted itself into strands and pillows and lifting smoke. What once was everything became something—first only fog moved over the water, then colors separated and emerged, win-ter wrens chattered, and small points of land defined themselves, one after another, unfolding down the river. The white-barked alder, the amber leaves—I watched the world recreate itself, sorting the light from the darkness, the waters above the firmament from the waters below, the seas from the dry land, the day from the night, humans from marshland and mud and this tidewater island, a heap of gray stones that comes and goes with the tide.

I could hear boats approaching long before they came into view, simple boats with old motors puttering upstream, the smell of gasoline mixing with damp mud and deep water, little motorboats pushing bow waves against the tide. Three men usually, sometimes a dog, or two men and a boy, they stood in the boat, because no one wants to sit on a fog-slicked deck and soak their pants. The question was always the same, called across the water: *Salmon rolling?* And the answer was always the same: *Not here.*

Maybe the salmon are slow in coming this year. Maybe they have already pushed upstream or are holding in the estuary, waiting for rain. Maybe they are in a different river, bank to bank in the Alsea or the Yaquina or the Trask, fanning their fins in strips of light falling through old-growth fir. Maybe they won't come this year, I thought, imagining that the salmon decided to stay at home, the way I like to pretend that my parents are asleep in their house in a different time zone, holding hands the way they did, blanket falling off one edge of the bed, light coming through the slats of the blinds, the striped light.

What no one would say, maybe what no one could imagine, was that maybe the last salmon of this run had died, and fall salmon would not run in this river again. And maybe that wasn't true. Maybe they *were* waiting for rain. Maybe they were just not jumping. How do you

know if there are salmon in the slack water, until you
hear the thud, and you turn in time to see a bright splash
and a broad back curling into a deep black-water eddy.

Our sleeping bags would never dry on this damp
island. Frank stuffed them wet and stowed them under
the deck. He hadn't caught any salmon, hadn't seen any,
hadn't heard a salmon roll. We floated downriver on the
ebbing tide, rowing close to the sandy beaches, trying
to read stories in the footprints of raccoons and otters
that wandered along the edge, also looking for salmon.
On a sandbar, we saw where an otter had hauled itself
up, dripping, shaken itself—the little circles in the sand,
like prints of raindrops—and then dragged its tail up
the beach.

The otter's tracks led to the edge of the grass. We
beached the boat and followed the tracks to the huge
corpse of a bright salmon, heavy as an amputated leg.
Her head had been cut off and taken away. We rolled
her over. Someone had slit her belly, gills to anus, and
taken the eggs—those thick slabs of red eggs. The rest
of the fish was left to rot, to turn to slime and sink into
the earth. Small animals had gnawed at the edges of
the salmon's gut, but the otter had left it alone, probably
smelling the metal knife that slit the fish, the boots that
walked away and left her in the sand.

And somewhere there was a fisherman using those
eggs as bait to fish for salmon. In my mind's eye, I watch
him set the egg mass oozing on his yellow-slicked knee,
cut a thumb-size chunk, drive a barbed hook through
the piece, loop the heavy line around the eggs, check to

make sure his bobber is tight, and then hurl the eggs to
the far side of the pool, where they sink into the shadows
below the ferns, down near the rocks, in still water, where
they hang, the bright-red hook-embedded eggs, in a pool
where there are no more salmon.

I tried to keep the boat out of the shadows, but the
sun was low, often behind the trees, and there wasn't
much light left on the river even in mid-afternoon.
Between sun and shade, the difference in temperature
was remarkable—summer and winter, T-shirt and fleece
jacket. I switched from baseball cap to wool hat, and
back and forth around each corner. More small boats
motored past us, cutting their engines in quiet water, listening for rolling salmon.

If this river's salmon run is finally extinct, what will
we have lost? What difference does it make? What is the
value of a salmon—these salmon, on this river? I suppose
that people can buy Alaskan salmon, getting cheaper
every year. Fishermen can watch football on Saturday
afternoons instead of fishing, and football's been good
this fall in Oregon—the Beavers and the Ducks both
winning for the first time in years. Rain will still fall on
quiet pools, and fog will still rise, and if there are fewer
raccoons and otters, if there are sparser trees, there will
still be amber leaves sluicing onto the black water, and
the smell of damp river and cutover forests. And how
many people get down to the river anyway? What is a
salmon to a person who's never seen one roll?

Slack high tide. The salmon hole just before the take-
out ramp is always full of fishermen, letting their boats

drift in the back eddies, trolling with flashers, lingering with the last lingering light, not eager to make the transition from water to land, from river to parking lot, from rowing a boat to backing a trailer into traffic. There was still some light behind the alders, but one after another, fishermen stood in their boats to pull heavy sweaters over their heads, holding their poles with their knees.

Maybe a pulse of salmon would swim through, salmon that had been waiting for high tide before they pushed from the sea to the land, from the dark ocean to the light-filled streams, our own Persephone, from darkness to light each year, to mark the seasons passing. From water to air and down again, salmon roll into this insubstantial world that will not support their weight, then sink back into water—a glimpse of cedars, sharp birdsong, and then the silted darkness—living and dying, from water to solid flesh and back to water again, a moist stain on a beach. Not creatures of the sea, not creatures of the river, not flesh, not fog: salmon are all of these— and the regular, rhythmic, reliable movement from one world to the other, our glimpse of the possibility of our own transformation. Salmon are our reminder that everything once was one thing and will be again, and we are part of that one big thing, separated only for a season.

FINIS / GENESIS

*If the world was created by the separation
of one thing from another, the seas from the dry land,
the birds of the air from the fish of the sea,
will it end with a gradual coming together?*

ON THE LAST DAY, a woman walked to the edge of
the water. Fog moved over the beach, and she became a
crouching man. When the mist lifted above the last of
the evening light, the man had turned to mud. In the
dusk, a heron perched on the mounded mud, and black-
clawed crabs and clam worms sheltered in its damp
hollows.

Beyond the point of land, two loons slowly slipped
below the surface of the water, and a cormorant banked
into the sea. The wings of the birds became fins and their
feathers became streaming silver spume, and they were
fish. Herring arced into the air and became winged birds
that flew above the earth.

In the fog-shrouded sunset, the last half-dome of the
sun was the waning moon, splashed by dark waves. Then
the moon faded into night. Days softened into years, and

years passed in a single day. The seasons merged into one another, yellow alder leaves melting holes in the ice, ice melting into fawn lilies, faded and pocked as old snow.

And tidewater crept into the eelgrass swales and spilled into the black-water streams and into all the dark spaces gathered together in tumbled headlands. When the tide sank again, it pulled down the sticks and the silt and the smooth stones. Rising and sinking, the seas mixed with the dry land, with the disappearing islands and silent stones, and the islands sifted into the sea. In the surge and drifting mist, the waters below lifted into the waters above. And under the clouds there was no starlight or moonlight or sunlight, but a yellow glow pouring onto the purple skin of the sea.

Then, there was no light and there was no darkness, only a shining slick on the swell, the spirit of God moving upon the face of the waters, flickering in the wind riffles, rising and sinking, in this time before the evening and the morning of the first day.

THE NIGHT OF THE RAZOR-CLAM TIDE

SHOVELS OVER OUR SHOULDERS and buckets in our hands, we hiked through beach-grass hummocks, heading for the sea. The day was cold and overcast, with a south wind so strong it bent the grass to the ground and raised ripples on the puddles in the trail. But this was good—the weather seemed to be keeping everyone else at home, probably finishing off the brandy and pumpkin pie, putting another log on the fire, wishing maybe they hadn't eaten so much. Out in the dunes, it was only us, bending into the wind, hurrying to get to the beach an hour before the razor-clam tide, a minus tide, the lowest tide in November. This was a family trip, as Thanksgiving celebrations should be—Jon and Frank and I, and my sister and her husband, and their daughter, Carley—six of us thumping along in tall boots through the clean, wild wind.

We followed the trail to the top of the foredune and stared down at the beach. There must have been a thousand people—pickup trucks parked every which way on the sand, dogs running around, people formed up into a crowd wavering along the edge of the sea, the whole flock of them running inland as each wave slid in, then scuttering seaward behind the receding line of foam. We stood for a moment, trying to figure out where all these people came from. How did they get their cars onto the beach, and why weren't they home watching football? Then we took great leaping steps down the dune and joined the crowd.

There was a man in an oxford-cloth shirt, looking like he'd just yanked off his tie, thrown it into the backseat, pulled on camouflage waders, and walked into the sea. There was a bearded man in a slicker and shorts, with his leg hair plastered to his skin. A woman shuffled around in neoprene waders so big that the crotch fell to her knees and the feet flopped behind her like broken legs. Two little boys ran by in high boots, chased by the surge, then back they ran, kicking at the line of foam as the water sank into the sea.

Suddenly low sun broke through the clouds. Thin lines of light shot between the leaping waves, and the people burst into color—red and yellow and blue and more yellow, all reflected in the wet mirror of the beach. Sunbeams spotlighted the yellow slickers, the red raincoats, the blue parkas, the shiny black boots, and the brilliant, sharp-edged reflections.

Each time the slick of water rose and receded, people followed it seaward. They each carried a shovel turned upside down, so the handle pointed toward the sand. They walked a few steps, thumped the sand with the handles of their shovels, walked a little farther, thumped again, hoping to see a dimple form in the sand. That dimple would mark the place where a clam flinched at the disturbance and pulled back its siphons, leaving a hollow hole.

Merging into the line of people, we wandered up and down the beach, thumping and watching. A shout went up and we turned sideways to brace against an oversize, onrushing wave. The wave lifted a rooster tail against our calves, then rushed on with a force like a river. It washed the legs out from under a middle-aged woman. She rolled in the surf, scrambling to her feet. Children raced up the beach. We stood up to our boot tops in water that calmed, then slowly ebbed toward the sea. We walked on, thumping and watching.

And then the sun was at the horizon, huge, lemon yellow, only partially visible behind suddenly golden-rimmed clouds. Everyone looked up from their digging, and just then the next wave caught the children and filled their boots and knocked them laughing on their yellow-slickered bottoms. Forgetting their shovels and their search, everyone turned toward the sunset and watched the foam lift off the surf—the white waves, the gold-tipped clouds, the impossible sun sinking so fast we could see it go. And then it was gone and the world turned silver, even the children, shining like fish in the mist.

Frank drove his shovel into the sand, sinking it to the shaft on the seaward side of a dent. He dropped to his knees, reached past his elbows into the watery sand, and brought up a razor clam. It was big, longer than his hand, and so fat it couldn't close its shell—a pound of clam, sweet and white and clean and smelling of the sea.

People wandered all over the wet flats in the darkening day, leaning on their shovels, tapping the sand, abruptly dropping to their knees. Pale fog hid the base of the headlands. As the dusk got darker and colder, some gathered up their families and left the beach, their headlights making a wide sweep across the sand. There would be clams for a late Thanksgiving dinner in their houses, butter sizzling and salty sea smell steaming the windows.

Other people lit kerosene lanterns and stayed on. Up and down the beach, we could see circles of yellow light swinging, and answering balls of light reflected on the slick of the ebbing tide. The darker the seas got, the more deeply blue the sky grew, and the first stars started to appear. Black-silhouetted people gathered around their lanterns, slowly moving together across the strand, watching the sand for a sign, their faces glowing and the fronts of their rubber overalls slick and glistening in lantern light—red, yellow, blue. They stood up to their shins in the black sea, lanterns swinging over the shallows, a wash of bright color swirling around their knees.

When the seas poured out again, I saw the sand slump into a little dent. I pushed in my shovel and wiggled it back and forth. Then I got down on my knees, jammed my sleeve up to my elbow, and plunged my hand into cold sand. Carefully, to keep from cutting my fingers, I groped around. Something flinched. I closed my hand around a clam and brought it up with a shout that disappeared in the thudding surf. Brown-blue opalescent clams lay in the bottom of our buckets. Two for each of us, all so fat we didn't need any more.

I think I know what it means to be blessed. The empty sand, the sudden sign, and then the fat sweet clam—unseen, undeserved, enough. And I'm starting to see what it means to be grateful.

When I question Western philosophy about gratitude, I get a thin, dry answer: To be grateful is to feel kindly toward a benefactor, something one ought to do, but an imperfect duty, because no one can demand it from another. Like forgiveness or love, gratitude has to come freely or it loses its worth. Fair enough, but how can anyone help but be grateful on a night like the night of the razor-clam tide? To be alive to the damp wind and the laughter of children, to feel the pressure of the sea against your boots and the weight of clams in your bucket—this is enough, a great gift. And is this night so different from any other night?

I'm beginning to understand that gratitude is a way of life.

Gratitude is a kind of seeing, an awareness of the magnitude of the gift of this earth. To see the world gratefully is to be endlessly surprised by the bare fact of it, its beauty and power and everlastingness. Gratitude is attentiveness. It's easy to move through the world and never notice how a shifting wind changes the air from salt to cedar, easy to overlook the invisible moon that moves the tides. To be grateful is to stand with stinging eyes and reddening nose in the northwest wind, taking it in—really this, taking it in—the expanse of dunes and dusk and each blade of beach grass drawing a circle on the sand. Gratitude peels the brown flakes from a clam shell and holds it into the sun—the violet glow—and wonders at the ridges on the shell, one for every year, so much like the ripples in creek beds on the beach.

Gratitude is also a kind of terror. The gifts of this world come unbidden and undeserved. Humankind has no claim against the universe for starlight or clams. No one owes us any of this—the air to breathe, the children to fear for, the tides to mark each day, the winter storms. Rain is not a birthright. The world is contingent, improbable, beyond our control: it could be, or not. A small change in a constant, and none of this happens— not the universe, not the clams. If it were to be taken away, there is nothing we could do to get it back, no entitlement we could claim. The gift is a mystery, beyond understanding—why there is something, rather than nothing, and why it is so beautiful.

Gratitude is a kind of rejoicing. Even though it might not have been and may yet not be, the earth is. The sudden awareness of the gift can fill us with joy, a well-being that arrives like high tide, lifting our spirits, expanding our sense of possibility, spreading out calm and shining at the horizons of our lives.

And is gratitude a moral obligation? I would say it is. The obligation is owed to the earth itself. To be grateful is to live a life that honors the gift. To care for it, keep it safe, protect it from damage. Not to discount or ignore it, but to use it respectfully. To celebrate it, to honor the worth of it in a thousand ways, not just in words, but in how we live our lives.

THE CHRISTMAS STORY

THIS YEAR, WE FLED CHRISTMAS. All of us, Frank and I and our grown kids, packed up and flew to Costa Rica, away from the fir trees topped with angels, south to the black vultures and iguanas. After so many years, Christmas was getting hard. "What do you want for Christmas?" my son and daughter would ask me, while I stewed about what I might give them. How can a present tell your children what you want for them? In retrospect, maybe I was hoping that a black vulture would do that job, would say, here in this sun-glazed sea, in the flecks of blue and gold that dart through underwater shadows, in the howl of monkeys in the morning and the tracks of hermit crabs on the beach, here is the measure of how much I love you and hope for you.

Or maybe it wasn't about hope. This winter has been a dark time, darker than usual, the world gone awry and the government hardening us for war on nations, war on terrorism, war on forests, war on just about everything. So maybe our decision was more about fear than hope. For whatever reason, we decided not to do Christmas this year. Christmas Eve found us sitting in the dark on the steps of the building at the entrance to the *Parque Nacional Marino Las Baulas de Guanacaste,* waiting.

We waited for hours at the national park head-quarters, watching geckos hunt around the porch lights, snapping up fruit flies and mosquitos. Geckos are splay-toed little lizards with enormous eyes. We watched them dart up walls and across ceilings, sticking tight with micro-scopic suction cups at the ends of hairs on their toes. Geckos click like clocks to claim a territory, a prime spot behind the light switch, the corner of a beam. *Geck-o geck-o,* they marked time passing, loud over the shriek of katydids and the voices of people draped across the steps, speaking quietly in languages I didn't understand.

A mother sprayed insect repellent in her child's hair. A teenager read a book in German. A couple broke away to get dinner at the restaurant next door, making someone else promise to fetch them if something hap-pened. The rest of us waited. Now and then, a shortwave radio crackled with the sound of men speaking urgently in Spanish and everyone stood up. But when nothing changed, we settled back into our conversations and our books.

Then suddenly, a park ranger appeared, counted off fif-teen people, and led us down the road to the beach. Word had come that a leatherback turtle had climbed out of the sea and was plowing across the beach to dig a nest.

The night had been densely dark back up the road, but when we emerged from the forest trail, the ocean was luminous, throwing back the light of a million stars. The sand was black, as strewn with white shells as the sky was strewn with stars. Five miles across the bay, lights from Tamarindo lit a streak of rosy water. Other than that, no lights marred the wildness of the beach, not a flashlight or porchlight, not a fire. We walked single file, finding our way in the dark by following the white rim of the breakers. Not sure where we were, not sure how far we would have to go, we trudged along in silence. My feet began to chafe from walking in sand. But then the radio spoke urgently, and our little group stopped. The turtle had laid her eggs and returned to the sea. We would wait on the beach until another turtle swam to shore.

We lay on the sand with our hands clasped behind our heads and watched the night. I want to tell what it meant to me, to lie on that wild beach with my husband and our grown-up children, together again in that darkness, in that warm air. We could hear the quiet surge of the sea and sometimes the scratching of ghost crabs. Stars reflected on the wet strand—not points of light, but streaks pointing toward the beach, as if sand knew something about starlight we could only imagine. There was the smell of salt-dampened sand, and just a hint of skunk. Sometimes, a lightning bug flashed. I said to myself, hold on to this. Float on the joy of it. Feel the embrace of this little family. This will not happen again in your lifetime.

The wind blew onshore, but we were warm. Sometimes a star would fall, really fall, tumbling straight down to the pale surf: a thousand degrees of shining, and the white and red lights of resorts at Tamarindo just a glitter on the bay. I could feel my children next to me, as I had not felt their physical presence since they were small.

An hour went by, maybe more. Then we saw a red light approaching from down the beach, and we were on our feet and moving again. Before long, we crossed the path of the leatherback turtle that had nested earlier that night.

A leatherback may swim a thousand miles across the Pacific, but she always returns to lay her eggs on the beach where she was born. Holding offshore, she waits for high tide. I think of the terrible urgency, the weight of a hundred eggs ripening in her belly, the pressure to deliver them to a place the tide can't reach. I think how desperately I would plow through the surf to the beach, and how heavy my body would feel in the sudden gravity, the weight of the world pressing me into soft sand. The track on the beach was wide and deep—four feet wide, four inches deep, as if someone had tied a rope to a front door, wrestled a boulder on top of it, and dragged it up the beach. We knelt on the sand and measured the track with our hands.

Nine years ago, 1,400 turtles nested on this beach. Last year, there were 68. Biologists blame the bycatch, turtles caught on lines and nets meant for fish. Worse, turtles instinctively swim toward light—the luminous rim of the breakers. So artificial lights from resort developments confuse them and lure them to all the wrong places, another grave danger. Although new For

Sale signs crowd every path to this park, the beach is three and a half kilometers of darkness, so far saved from artificial light.

We walked on silently, our way marked by stars reflected on wet sand left by receding waves. I don't understand this, how the star itself is a point of light and its reflection is an arrow.

Before long, our group stopped abruptly at another, fresher track. Following the park ranger, we turned up the beach, moving slowly now, still silently, climbing through dry sand. And there, on the dune above the high tide line, was the turtle, vaguely red in the light of the ranger's flashlight. She was bigger than I thought she would be—maybe three feet wide, four feet long. Her back was dark and shiny, like varnished leather, with deep lengthwise folds. Using her hind flippers, she was digging a hole in the sand, not just shoving the sand out of the way, but curling a back flipper into a scoop and lifting out sand, cupful by cupful, slowly.

We came up behind her and gathered in small clusters, wanting to see her, but unwilling to go too close. If anyone spoke at all, it was in whispers. At first people stood eagerly and strained forward to see in the dark. A man lifted his son to his shoulders. But as the turtle dug and dug, one by one the people dropped to their knees, until we are all on our knees, waiting for this birth. Above the dark and breeze-swept beach, the silent stars move slowly across the black fabric of the sky. The wind rises, lifting dry sand. A red flashlight beam streams its light on the turtle's huge back, and we, who have come so far, keep watch.

An hour goes by, maybe more. The turtle digs more and more slowly, and finally stops half suspended over the opening in the sand. The attending biologists talk urgently and quietly among themselves. Then one of them kneels by the hole and starts to dig. Red lights flash over the turtle's back and reflect off the sand, as more biologists gather with their flashlights. Something has gone terribly wrong. The turtle finally heaves herself away from the hole, drags her body over the berm of the high tide line, and lumbers the long way back to the sea.

I don't know what sign, what facts recorded in that ancient brain, warned her not to entrust her eggs to the world in this place, in this time. I don't know when the world will be worthy of the hope in a leatherback turtle heavy with eggs. All I know is that there will be no eggs in this nest. A biologist whispers in Spanish. Someone translates: She might try again. But probably not. Somewhere in the sea, she will release the eggs, and they will sink, one by one, soft and white, down into the darkness of the ocean, the dark steep falling, and they will die.

🐚

IF YOU FLOAT ON YOUR BACK in the swimming pool at the *pensione,* you look up into the white face of a papier-mâché snowman. He's wearing reflective sunglasses and a fake carrot nose. His smile is painted on with black tempera paint and he has a cardboard top hat. Past him, in the blue sky, black vultures are soaring. This is a good way to watch vultures, floating on your back. I tip my wings as they tip theirs, and float on water the same temperature as the sun-scorched sky. A flock of green parrots rushes by, screeching.

Out in the parking lot, someone has built a crèche in a shed made of hay bales covered with sheet metal. Mary is a blue shower curtain stuffed with straw. Her face is drawn on with a marking pen—a wan smile, two wide eyes. Joseph's face is a pillowcase stuffed with cotton. Cotton balls bulge out the bottom in a disheveled beard. A wren stands on Joseph's shoulder, pulling out cotton for its nest. I saw the wren's nest at breakfast; in a tangle of grass and cotton balls in the crook of a cactus's arm, Joseph's beard cradled three tiny pink eggs. There may or may not be a Jesus in the manger; I can't see in. But it does have ants, swarming over the splayed leg of a dead katydid. This is what we hear at night, the piping of katydids in the trees, and in the mornings, we hear monkeys woofing, like big dogs.

"Did anyone see her face?" I'm standing up in the pool. It has suddenly occurred to me that in all the hugeness of the mother turtle's back, with all our hopes concentrated on her fleshy tail, I had never seen her eyes or the expression on her face. "No," Jonathan says, "but if we'd have looked, we probably could have seen tears in her eyes."

"Turtles cry," he says flatly. "It's how they get rid of the salt in the water they drink."

How could we not have looked for the expression on her face?

I HAD BEEN UP before dawn on Christmas Day, walking the road back toward the beach on feet still stinging from the nighttime hike. This far south, dawn is brilliant and hot. The road is dusty and strewn with roadkill—purple and orange land crabs, squashed flat, swarming with ants. Everything dead or dying swarms with ants in this country. Doves wander in the road, pecking at gravel, and call out from the electrical lines.

On the beach at six o'clock in the morning, strong young men and women stand looking out to sea, inspecting the green waves. Already a couple of people are surfing. I walk along the beach to look for signs of the night. New-dug holes of ghost crabs. Three-toed tracks from a large wading bird. Broken sand dollars. Finally I cross the track where the first leatherback plowed up from the sea—the turtle we never saw. I can clearly make out each lunge, the dug-in flippers, the tail stabbing into sand. She had climbed the loose steep face to the sand above high tide to lay her eggs—probably forty to sixty of them, small, like white lemons, and then a layer of infertile eggs to satisfy a fox or vulture. I don't know if there are any eggs here now. Someone told me the biologists catch them as they drop, put them in a cloth bag, and take them to the lab to raise. The sand was churned up in a depression twelve feet across. From there, her track circled back, gouging toward the sea, and disappeared in clean-washed sand.

I keep on walking. Here, the rubber head of a Minnie Mouse doll rolls in the surf. Her face is faded—who knows how long she's washed in and out with the tide—so all the color is scrubbed away. But she still has the startled eyes, the huge ears, the bow on her head, the wide smile. I prop her head upright in dry sand and leave her grinning out to sea.

A few paces farther, I come across a hatchling turtle, feebly crawling in the wrong direction. It isn't a leatherback; its back is crimped into leathery plates, not pleats. My best guess is an Olive Ridley, another turtle that nests on this beach. The tiny turtle is very weak, barely able to drag itself forward, and instead of clambering toward the sea, it is staggering along parallel to the ocean. I pick it up. It fits easily into the palm of my hand. It weighs exactly nothing. How could something that looks so dense be so light?—this tiny spark of turtle. Is there something I can offer to this baby, so small and so lost? Is there a reason why I shouldn't carry it to the sea? I think over the options. There's no mercy out beyond the surf. But a few more minutes in the sun, maybe a half hour, and it will surely be dead, sprinkled with sand, and an army of ants on the way.

I carry it to ankle-deep water and lay it down gently. It slowly sinks, washing side to side, like a leaf in a river. As a surge of water washes in, the turtle tumbles end over end and rolls back to shore. So I cradle it in my hands at the top of the water and lift it over each breaking wave. For a time, it rests in the bowl of my hands. Then it flippers up for a breath, flippers up again, and starts finning toward the sea. I open my hands. The turtle swims through the next surge, keeping its direction, and then it is gone.

ANOTHER WORLD COULD START RIGHT HERE

THE WORDS TO SONGS flap uncontrollably, like starlings, in my brain. *O for a thousand tongues to sing* in the parking lot on Cape Foulweather while a crow sneaks up on my sandwich. *How many roads must a man walk down* as I wait on the phone. *O beautiful for spacious skies,* at the grocery store, behind the bread. There are a thousand million things I don't remember from my childhood— my teachers' names, the shape of my father's hands—but I'll never forget Garfunkel's part for "The Sound of Silence," all four verses.

We sang standing up in church when my sister and I were children. This is what I remember, all the people in the congregation rising at the same time, and the sound we made, standing—a raucous creak as the benches relax, and the rasping of clothes and pages. The simultaneous rising-up, and then the miracle: A hundred, two hundred irreducibly individual people in the pews—the fierce grocery clerk and the school secretary, the sparrow-shouldered woman, the bobbing organist, the huge-purse ladies and the small-headed men, all with their secret plots and sorrows—all open their mouths at the same time. Ordinary air sucks past lips red or wine or pallid, and when the air blows back out of all those lungs, it has become one amazing, beautiful thing.

But now my sister says, "I don't sing as much as I used to, because, more and more, it makes me cry." I am astounded, because lately I have felt this way too. When I stand to sing—at a football game, for heaven's sake, or a kinder-garten holiday concert or in church—I might get through a word or two, *For the beauty of the earth, for the glory of the sky.* But then I have to stop singing, snuffling and embar-rassed, because crying takes all the air and nothing is left for the song. I am trying to understand this power in music.

Two decades ago, NASA scientists sent a spacecraft past Saturn, past Neptune, past Pluto, knowing that it would take a hard swing around the solar system and then wing into space and never stop, ever—unless beings from another place netted it and took it home. What message should the satellite carry to help space-faring strangers understand who we are? The scientists made a phonograph record—a twelve-inch copper disk in an aluminum jacket. They tucked a cartridge and needle into the satellite and drew a picture of how a record player works. Then they loaded the record with music: Bach and Beethoven and "Johnny B. Goode." African drums and Navajo night chants. Panpipes, bagpipes, *The Magic Flute*. "Go Johnny, Go," *Sing with all the sons of glory, Joy Joy Sisters and Brother*s, all tucked there in the satellite like an egg to be hatched, a seed to germinate, flying through dark space long after we have reduced our civilizations to stones.

Another world could start right there, seeding some strange sea with this one most glorious thing in the universe—the fact that human beings can take the vibration of the physical world, just that, just the trembling of the universe, and make it into the very expression of joy and thanksgiving.

How do we do it? I pester my husband because, with his PhD in neurobiology, he's supposed to know how the brain works. Instead of answering, he hands me an issue of a scientific magazine, folded open. It's a four-color picture of a cross section of the human brain, artificially colored magenta, yellow, green, and the intense blue of the ocean under a storm. There is no place in the brain especially for music, scientists have discovered, the way there is a special place for smell or sight. The aquamarine light of music floods through the brain, pooling in all the places where we feel, understand, remember, prefer, perceive, analyze, hope, and fear. The part of the brain that reads music helps us read pain in a person's face. The place for perfect pitch is the same area the brain uses to understand language. We remember a melody in the place we remember our children's names. The splashing edges of this great blue sea of music are the places where understanding can grow.

So what goes wrong? Wouldn't you think that if we have the ability to bring all this together to create harmony out of thin air, we could find a way to live in harmony too? You can't really blame NASA scientists for not telling the whole heartbreaking story, laying it out for the grieving universe to know. Humankind comes so close. Again and again, we almost find a way to live together like a song, all the parts flowing down their own paths and converging into something perfect and powerful. Sometimes, in small ways, we actually do it—a neighborhood, a garden, a concert, a class. And then, again and again, we fail: a small meanness or prolonged war, a lonely child or a poisoned river. This is the sorrow in the heart of all music.

All the same, I know what it means to sing standing up, and I try to remember what I have to do to live my life like music. Taut and attentive, to hum with the energy of the world outside my door—the sloshing tides and grieving parents and rising winds. Standing with strangers, to listen to their voices and tune myself to what is beautiful in them, and true. And sometimes, to walk to the very edge of my life and stand on the rim with my hair blowing back and my voice raised in celebration—the "Ode to Joy," barreling past Saturn.

A physicist will tell you what you already know. That harmony has the power to shake the world. Sing one clear note, and the same tone will hum in the window glass, in the electric wires, in the neighbor's piano, in the pine needles, and the air will be changed forever.

At the coast with my sister, in wind so strong it almost flattens us, we fight our way to the top of the headland. There somebody, some astounding park official, has posted a sign with the words from Alfred, Lord Tennyson's poem "Crossing the Bar." *Twilight and evening bell, and after that the dark.* How many years ago did we sing that song with a church choir? "Do you remember?" I ask my sister, and of course she does. We stand in the protection of the lighthouse and try to sing, but cry instead in the perfect joining of headland and poetry, and wind and rain and sorrow, sisters and the surging sea.

ACKNOWLEDGMENTS

WHERE DO YOU GET YOUR IDEAS? It's the first
question people ask me in writing workshops. A writer's
good fortune is to live in a world swirling with ideas.
All a writer has to do is pull them out of the air and
convince them to line up on a page. Who could claim
the ideas for her own? They wing in from a thousand
directions—overheard conversations, suggestions from
friends, a cherished book, a dentist-office magazine,
memories, a student's question, the view across a lake,
a scientist's story, a sudden similarity, a public talk,
carefully argued.

The world's wealth of ideas is a great gift to a writer,
gratefully received. There are people of wisdom whose
ideas particularly inspire and move me—Rachel Carson,
Viola Cordova, Jim Dodge, Jack Forbes, Linda Hogan,
Freeman House, Oscar Kawagley, Robert Kennedy, Aldo
Leopold, Nel Noddings, Scott Russell Sanders, Gary
Snyder, Henry David Thoreau, Terry Tempest Williams,

Ann Zwinger. With gratitude and humility, I acknowledge their gifts and those of uncountable others.

I'm grateful to the scientists who shared their stories about the earth—Jack Dymond, Stan Gregory, Frank Lake, Frank Moore, Jonathan Moore, Fred Swanson, Allen Throop—and to my musician friends, John Bliss, Rachelle McCabe, and Libby Roderick. Credit goes to David Allen Sibley, whose beautiful transcriptions of birdsongs appear in these essays. Thanks to the writers, who took time from their own work to help to shape this book—Chris Anderson, Bill Cherwonit, Carole Ann Crateau, Franz Dolp, Jack Dymond, Charles Goodrich, Steve Radosevich, Carolyn Servid, Gail Wells. Thanks to my colleagues in philosophy—Marcus Borg, Courtney Campbell, Michael Nelson, and Lani Roberts. Warm thanks to all my students, and especially to Carrie Bailey, Francesca Marcus, Peter Martin, and Laura Schmidt.

Thanks to Emilie Buchwald, an editor of wisdom and wit, who could have retired to her gardens, but stayed on to finish this book; and to H. Emerson Blake and Hilary Reeves, the brilliant new leaders of Milkweed Editions. Thanks are due to the Hundere Endowment for Religion and Culture at Oregon State University, for grant support, and to the Spring Creek Project for Ideas, Nature, and the Written Word.

I'm grateful to my children, Erin Moore, Jonathan Moore, and Anne Carlson; and to my sisters, Nancy Rosselli and Sally Swegan. What would I do without their stories and their counsel, their ideas and wisdom, their songs, their love? And finally, thank you especially to my husband, Frank, who, risking the dangers of freezing and drowning and faith, traveled half the earth in the rain, keeping the boat afloat.

KATHLEEN DEAN MOORE is a professor of philosophy at Oregon State University. She is the author of *Riverwalking* and *Holdfast*, which received the Sigurd Olson Nature Writing Award. Moore is frequently called on to speak at conferences and conventions where the work of conservation is discussed. Her writings are widely influential and she has been honored by Oregon State University as a Distinguished Professor. She is the mother of two grown children and lives with her husband in the Pacific Northwest.

MORE BOOKS ON

THE WORLD AS HOME

FROM

MILKWEED ⬤ EDITIONS

To order books or for more information, contact Milkweed at (800) 520-6455
or visit our Web site (www.worldashome.org).

Toward the Livable City
Edited by Emilie Buchwald

Wild Earth:
Wild Ideas for a World Out of
Balance
Edited by Tom Butler

The Book of the Everglades
Edited by Susan Cerulean

Swimming with Giants:
My Encounters with Whales,
Dolphins, and Seals
Anne Collet

The Prairie in Her Eyes
Ann Daum

The Colors of Nature:
Culture, Identity, and the
Natural World
*Edited by Alison H. Deming and
Lauret E. Savoy*

Boundary Waters:
The Grace of the Wild
Paul Gruchow

Grass Roots:
The Universe of Home
Paul Gruchow

The Necessity of Empty Places
Paul Gruchow

A Sense of the Morning:
Field Notes of a Born Observer
David Brendan Hopes

Arctic Refuge:
A Circle of Testimony
*Compiled by Hank Lentfer and
Carolyn Servid*

This Incomparable Land:
A Guide to American Nature
Writing
Thomas J. Lyon

A Wing in the Door:
Life with a Red-Tailed Hawk
Peri Phillips McQuay

The Barn at the End of the
World: The Apprenticeship of a
Quaker, Buddhist Shepherd
Mary Rose O'Reilley

MILKWEED EDITIONS

Founded in 1979, Milkweed Editions is the largest independent, nonprofit, literary publisher in the United States. Milkweed publishes with the intention of making a humane impact on society, in the belief that good writing can transform the human heart and spirit. Within this mission, Milkweed publishes in five areas: fiction, nonfiction, poetry, children's literature for middle-grade readers, and the World As Home—books about our relationship with the natural world.

The World As Home is dedicated to exploring and expanding our relationship with the natural world. These books are a forum for distinctive writing that alerts the reader to vital issues and offers personal testimonies to living harmoniously with the world around us.

JOIN US

Milkweed depends on the generosity of foundations and individuals like you, in addition to the sales of its books. In an increasingly consolidated and bottom-line driven publishing world, your support allows us to select and publish books on the basis of their literary quality and the depth of their message. Please visit our Web site (www.milkweed.org) or contact us at (800) 520-6455 to learn more about our donor program.

Interior design by Christian Fünfhausen.
Typeset in 11/15 point Adobe Caslon.